Social Protection in Islamic Law

Ayten Vahapoğlu Erol

Social Protection In Islamic Law

Theoretical Perspective

PETER LANG

Bibliographic Information published by the Deutsche Nationalbibliothek
The Deutsche Nationalbibliothek lists this publication in the Deutsche
Nationalbibliografie; detailed bibliographic data is available online at
http://dnb.d-nb.de.

Library of Congress Cataloging-in-Publication Data
A CIP catalog record for this book has been applied for
at the Library of Congress.

ISBN 978-3-631-75913-4 (Print)
E-ISBN 978-3-631-75914-1 (E-PDF)
E-ISBN 978-3-631-75915-8 (EPUB)
E-ISBN 978-3-631-75916-5 (MOBI)
DOI 10.3726/b14266

© Peter Lang GmbH
Internationaler Verlag der Wissenschaften
Berlin 2018
All rights reserved.

Peter Lang – Berlin · Bern · Bruxelles · New York ·
Oxford · Warszawa · Wien

This publication has been peer reviewed.

www.peterlang.com

To my husband, Professor Turan Erol for his support and love.

Preface

It is known that throughout history, humans have encountered physiological and demographic risks originating from either their own behaviors or from external factors such as natural disasters, pandemic diseases, wars, awful treatment towards people of different religions and races, incidences of terror, and the waves of migration, demographic changes, and destabilization of the family structure that occur as a result of these. In addition to this, socioeconomic risks such as unemployment and poverty that come about together with the growth and recession in the nature of the free market economy, especially the crises that have shaken the economy of the world in which we live in recent years, and globalization. Income distribution has deteriorated even further because of the accumulation of capital in the hands of a limited section in national and international dimensions. Therefore, in periods of economic fluctuation, stagnation, and crisis, the low-income groups getting by with their labor will have an unavoidable need for additional support in the destitute situations they have succumbed to because of unemployment and loss of income. This need was even observed in developed European nations in the most recent period of global economic and financial crisis.

Social security is indispensable in dealing with these diverse risks and threats for every individual and society. Off course, many scholars around the world have been undertaking extensive researches and proposing solutions and policies for this purpose.

To achieve the social security goal globally, which is as old as the human existence, it is critical to know the principles, approaches and points of views of Islamic law regarding human being, property and life, and to adopt these principles in practice. We argue that these principles are universal and encompassing for the whole humanity and their wellbeing.

The shared values, according to Islamic law, that are the minimum conditions of living in a society and that humanity must preserve are those consisting of the protection of religion, life, reason, property, and lineage (külliyetü'l-hamse), and are evaluated in the scope in which religion aims to protect and maintain (makâsıdü'ş-şerîa'). Ensuring individual and communal welfare and order at the highest level by guaranteeing these and carrying out social justice and social protection in society by removing all kinds of evil, deviation, and corruption have been deemed the duty that must be fulfilled by believers, and thus, social protection has been evaluated in the scope of social policy. In this context, it aims to ensure social solidarity and social justice in society by encouraging mutual cooperation and solidarity for a life to be realized together as a society among its members, and at the same time, recognizing the theoretic direction of social protection in Islamic law, seen as one of the conditions upon which belief that has institutionalized must absolutely be founded upon carries great importance.

In our book, with reference to the fact that the issue of "Social Protection in Islamic Law" possesses multifaceted contents and a scope that would fit in volumes, we aimed to create awareness regarding the implementation of the fundamental principles and approaches that individuals and societies must internalize for the development of social protection in society according to Islamic Law, and to contribute to the search today for social protection.

The humble contribution that this work, which we able to complete with the grace and blessing of the Almighty Lord, will make to the world of science will be our source of happiness. The effort is ours, the success is God's.

Ayten Vahapoğlu Erol

Contents

Abbreviations 13

Introduction 15

1 Conceptual Framework of Social Protection in
  Islamic Law 21
  I   The Definition of Social Protection in Islamic Law 21
  II   The Subject of Social Protection in Islamic Law 26
  III   The Importance of Social Protection in Islamic Law 30
  IV   The Purpose of Social Protection in Islamic Law 36
  V   The Scope of Social Protection in Islamic Law 42
  VI   The Basic Elements of Social Protection in Islamic Law 45

2 The Basic Approaches (Principles) of Social Protection
  in Islamic Law 61
  I   The Principle of Tawhid 62
  II   The Principle of Morality 64
  III   The Principle of Property 67
  IV   The Principle of Justice 70
  V   The Principle of Brotherhood 73

Conclusion 77

Bibliography 81

Abbreviations

IED: Islamic Encyclopedia of Diyanet
İLAM: Scientific Research Center
ILO: International Labor Organization
İSAM: Islamic Research Center
Lt. Co.: Limited Partner Corporation
p.:   page
pp.:   pages

Introduction

It is a well-known fact that all religions[1] and political-economic systems, regardless of whether they have divine origins within their historical processes, have given importance to social protection and developed policies directed at social protection.

In this context, social protection throughout the world is a piece of social policy on the national and global scale.[2] Social policy today, as a phenomenon of the 20th century and a systematic concept that developed economies use, possesses an identity of struggling with every issue that negatively affects societal life or that threatens the integrity of society.[3] Social policy expressed with the concept of social politics are preventive measures that aim to eliminate various social problems that generally occur in different social segments of society and to ensure and popularize the tranquility of the individual and society.[4] In addition to this, they are the entirety of the social practices arranged based on the disposition of humans and adopted moral values. Social policy aims to attain a health, peaceful, and just level of welfare in terms of the material and immaterial, for the individual and society, by taking measures that allow humans to live humanely, and by working to eliminate the problem of poverty.[5] In line with this objective, the provision of the social protection of individuals and society and the fair distribution of national income in society with a system of social protection, by considering the needs of individuals, are the basis of social policies.[6]

---

1 For detail, see Faruk Beşer, *Social Security in Islam*, Nûn, Publishing House, Istanbul 2016, 4th Edition, pp. 82–86; Süleyman Özdemir, "A New Understanding in the Provision of Social Welfare: "The Welfare Mix" and Welfare Providing Institutions", p. 102. http://eski.bingol.edu.tr/media/154992/dddtamami.pdf (15.10.2017)

2 Aysen Tokol, *Social Policy*, 2nd Edition, Uludağ University, Ceylan Publishing, Bursa 1997, p. 94; Hüseyin Akyıldız, *Social Security Law*, Süleyman Demirel University Publication No: 43, Faculty of Economics and Sciences, Isparta 2004, p. 6.

3 Ebru Sargın, The Contributions of Social Cooperation and Solidarity Foundations on a Country's Economy, Namık Kemal University Institute of Social Sciences, *Unprinted Graduate Thesis*, Tekirdağ 2017, p. 23.

4 Murtaza Köse, "The Concept of Social Policy and Ömer B. Abdülaziz's Social Policy", *Atatürk University Journal of the Divinity School*, Issue: 34, Erzurum 2010, p. 78.

5 Murtaza Köse, pp. 79–80.

6 Akyıldız, pp. 5–6.

In terms of social policy, social protection expresses a structure that won't make an individual dependent on somebody else within an understanding of mutual cooperation and solidarity in society for the purpose of protecting the weak and vulnerable in society.[7] In this context, the state tasked with ensuring a minimum level of living for its citizens, without exception, is a social state; and the state that ensures social justice, social welfare, and social protection in society and that respects the law is a social law state.[8] In this framework, the social state must take measures that ensure social justice, social solidarity, and social justice in society by regulating the network between individuals and employment so that they may harmonize with each other.

Adopting and supporting policies that ensure the protection of disadvantaged segments of society with individuals within the societal structure and in economic poverty who have a need for there to be a social state carry great importance. The necessity to protect those in society who are weak, vulnerable, and dependent on care has been codified and is the responsibility of the state for the continuity of the sociopolitical structures that the understanding of being a social state brings.[9]

It is the duty of the social state to produce concrete policies to both positively affect the levels of life of weak and low-income groups in socioeconomic terms and to protect and raise the levels of life that these individuals have reached through the regulations and institutions identified in the field of social protection. Because the socioeconomic conditions of individuals and societies needs to be directly proportional to social policies, and social just in society needs to be ensured by reflecting development, especially on needy individuals and families. Social justice, however, is possible with institutions and regulations of social protection that will actualize social protection services so that all individuals in society are equal and free both before the law and in political, economic, and social life.

In this framework, the understanding of the social state requires the realization of actions to ensure the happiness of society in many areas like health, educational, and vital needs, primarily the security of the society. This promotional understanding of the social state and the actions it materializes have evolved

---

7 Sargın, p. 24.
8 Mehmet Erdoğan, *Dictionary of Islamic Law and Legal Terminology*, Rağbet Publications, (Publication date and place not available), p. 410.
9 Sargın, p. 23.

into the understanding of a state that checks itself with time and that protects society.[10]

As a result of social protection a basic function of the social state, it will be possible to ensure the unity, cooperation, and solidarity of society, to increase the economic freedoms of all individuals in society, and to realize equality and justice in society. In a social law state, it is essential that citizens are able to live without falling below a certain level of living and are supported with social and economic rights. Because in a social law state, the right to benefit from programs implemented to increase the welfare of individuals is accepted as the basic right of citizenship.[11] Therefore, considering the economic, social, and political processes of today, the social law state is not a vehicle but is functional in terms of the results it produces. The development of the functions of the social law state in providing socioeconomic social protection will enable faster economic growth as well as greater social integrity and social justice.[12]

On the other hand, religions are not only systems of belief but also include social, political, economic, and legal fields that these systems specify.[13]

The religion of Islam, along with including beliefs and moral values, wholly assesses all aspects of life holistically, including the material, immaterial, intellectual, individual, and communal. Therefore, the religion of Islam calls for individuals and societies to be balanced and straightforward in all kinds of affairs.[14]

Islamic legal experts concurred on the matter where religious norms meet on the point of providing benefit, preventing harm, and obstructing evils in the world for people. They said that the purpose for the religion of Islam's sending forth are affairs,[15] or in other words, to protect those that carry out the things that

---

10 Ayça Çambel, *Social Poverty and Social Protection in the Era of Globalization*, Ege University Department of Economics, Faculty of Economic and Administrative Sciences Research Methods in Social Sciences, Izmir 2015, p. 2.

11 Serdar Yay, "The Social State in Turkey in the Historical Process", *Journal of 21st Century Education and Society*, III, Issue: 9, Winter 2014, pp. 148–149.

12 Recep Kapar, *Greater Social Protection for Social Justice*, II, National Social Policy Congress, Ankara (24–26 November 2006). (www.disk.org.tr), p. 9. (www.sosyalkoruma.net) (12.10.2017)

13 Nihat Temel, *Assistance as Social Security Institutions in the Quran*, Emre Press, Istanbul 2000, p. 165.

14 Muhammed Esed, *Manner of Administration in Islam*, Trans.: M. Beşir Eryarsoy, Yöneliş Publications, Istanbul, (publication date not available), p. 64.

15 Affairs *are generally defined as the acquisition of what is beneficial and the elimination of what is harmful in Islamic legal methodological works (def-i mefâsid celb-i menâfi'dir/ celb-i menfaat and def-i madarrat).* (Gazzâlî, Ebû Hâmid Muhammed b. Muhammed,

benefit society and to eliminate the matters that bring harm to people, in accordance with this.[16] The realization of this general purpose has been connected to the protection of humans in five absolute senses, including the protection of life,[17] the protection of intellect,[18] the protection of religion,[19] the protection of lineage,[20] and the protection of property.[21] Therefore, the absolute protection of these five universal values, regardless of belief, for social protection in individuals and society is imperative.

While there is no model of a standard social law state in Islam, religion, law, morals, and social order constitute the social dimension of Islamic law. A service state based in social welfare and a law state based in justice and equality are the two fundamental principles of the model of the Islamic social state that are defined as social Islam.[22]

---

el-Müstesfâ min İlmi'l-Usûl, (Publisher not available),vol. I-II, Beirut 1993, I/174, 179; Abdulvehhâb Hallâf, İlmu Usûli'l-Fıkh, Mektebetü'd-Da'veti'l-İslâmiyye, Şebâbü'l-Ezher, Egypt, p. 84; Bûtî, Muhammed Saîd Ramazan, *Davâbıtu'l-Maslaha fî'ş-Şerî'ati'l-İslâmiyye,* Müessesetü'r-Risâle, Beirut 1402/1982, p. 22; Abdülkerim Zeydan, el-*Veciz fi Usuli'l-Fıkıh,* Dersaâdet, Istanbul, (publication date not avaible), p. 236,240; ez-Zuhaylî, el-Vecîz fi Usûli'l-Fıkh, Dâru'l-Fıkh, Dımeşk-Suriye 1431/2010, p. 92; Ferhat Koca, "An Evaluation of Maslahat-ı Mürsele ve Necmeddin et-Tûfî's Views on this Issue in Islamic Law", *İLAM Journal of Research,* Issue: 1, (January–June 1996), I/ 93; İbn Âşûr, Muhammed Tâhir, *Philosophy of Islamic Law: The Problem of Purpose,* (Trans. Vecdi Akyüz,Mehmet Erdoğan), İz Publishing House, Istanbul 1996, p. 122–123).

16 İbn Kayyim, Abdullah b. Muhammed b. Ebi Bekr el-Cevziyye, (A.D. 751/1350), *İ'lâmu'l-Muvakkîn an Rabbi'l-Âlemîn,* I–VII, Dâru'l-İbn Cevziyye, Riyad 1423, I/61; İbn Abdisselâm, İzzüddîn Abdilazîz, *el-Kavâidu'l-Kübrâ (Kavâidü'l-Ahkâm fî Mesâlihi'l-Enâm (Kavâid),* Dâru'l-Kalem, Dımeşk (publication date not available), vol. (I–II), I/11–12; For detail, see Şükrü Özen, "İstislâh", *Islamic Encyclopedia of Diyanet,* XXIII, pp. 383–388; Yunus Vehbi Yavuz, "Interpreting Intent", *Journal of Islamic Legal Research,* Issue: 8, Mehir Foundation Publications, Konya 2006, pp. 41–78, pp. 45–46; Hadi Sağlam, "Methods That Provide Dynamism to Islamic Law in the Face of Modern Problems", p. 16. http://www.akademiktarih.com/tarih-anabilim-dal/2026-osmanlaratrmalar/osmanlkuki-yap/28845-cada-problemler-karisinda-slam-hukukunadnamzm-salayan-metotlar.html (22.05.2017)
17 Nisâ, 4/93; Mâide, 5/32.
18 Ahzâb, 33/72.
19 Bakara, 2/256; Kâfirûn, 109/76.
20 Furkan, 35/74.
21 Nisâ, 4/5.
22 Ali Fuat Akçapınar, http://www.mirathaber.com/ali-fuat-akcapinar-islamsiyasetindebir-sosyal-devlet-modeli-var-midir-22-467y.html (30.01.2018)

We see the principles that are applications of public social policy of modern social states for the establishment of social protection services[23] for disadvantaged social groups in the Medina Islamic State that the Prophet Muhammad founded as the head of state. The hadith of: "The property that a person leaves behind in their death belongs to their heirs. The burden (social protection) the person who leaves behind debt and an impoverished family, however, belongs to us (the state)"[24] of the Prophet Muhammad, regarding this matter, expressly demonstrates that the primary duties of Islamic states is service to social segments that need aid and support.[25]

Indeed, one of the objectives of Islamic law is: "To reform[26] so as to make dominant communal life, general security, justice among people, and the protection of reasonable freedoms. In order to be able to realize this objective, Islamic law has brought about a civil order that contains all principles of law necessary to establish a social life within a state, to regulate relationships of people with each other and with the administrative authority, and to protect private and individual rights along with general and social rights."[27] This order covers everything ranging from the instruction[28] of the social course of events of the soul, the heart, and the personality of the individual; the occurrence, regulation, and solidarity of the family; and its financial savings with economic relationships that increase the level of Islamic society.[29] Therefore, legal rules are at the core of the model of social Islam, and should these rules be made valid in political, economic, and

23 For detail, see Fatıma Zeynep Belen, "Immaterial and Psychosocial Practices of Care for Disadvantaged Groups: The Example of Sevilla", *Immaterial and Psychosocial Care for Disadvantaged Groups*, Editors: İhsan Çapçıoğlu,Fatıma Zeynep Belen, Grafiker Publications, Ankara 2016, pp. 15–36.

24 Ebû Abdillâh Muhammed b. İsmâîl, *Sahihu'l-Buhârî*, el-Mektebetü'l-İslâmiyye, İstanbul (publication date not available), Kitabu'l-Ferâiz, 85, Bab: 4, p. 5.

25 Ali Fuat Akçapınar, http://www.mirathaber.com/ali-fuat-akcapinar-islam-siyasetinde-bir-sosyal-devlet-modeli-var-midir-22-467y.html (30.01.2018)

26 Hûd, 11/88.

27 Hayreddin Karaman, *Islamic Law in the Face of New Developments*, İz Publishing House, Istanbul 2004, p. 15; Ayten Erol, "The Societal Change And Progression Methodology of Islamic Law in Relation to Maslahah", Editor: Ayten Erol, *Maslahat in Islamic Sciences*, Gece Kitaplığı Publishing House, Ankara 2017, (pp. 13–39), p. 13

28 See Muhammed Ali Yazıbaşı, "Moral Education and Instruction from Classical Ottoman to II. Mesrutiyet Period in Ottoman", *Journal of Human and Societal Sciences Research*, 3, 2014, Issue: 4, (pp. 761–780), p. 763, 764.

29 Abdullah Ulvân, *Social Solidarity in Islam*, Trans.: İsmail Kaya, Uysal Bookstore, Sebat Ofset Press, Konya 1985, p. 30

social life, the social rights of people will have been protected and an ideal society of solidarity, in which there is no unfair competition, will have occurred.[30]

The world view of the religion of Islam for social life and social problems is the social policy of Islam. In other words, we can say that the theoretic and practical provisions that the religion of Islam recommends for social policy, social justice, and social protection constitute the social orientation of the religion of Islam.

As a matter of fact, along with civil and political rights, the social and economic rights of people must be defined as a necessity of being human, and social protection must be realized, in the provision of social justice.[31]

Our book attempts a theoretical perspective of social protection in Islamic law and comprises two sections apart from the preface and introduction. In the first section of our book, we tried to lay down the conceptual framework of social protection in Islamic law such as definition, importance and pillars; and in the second section, we tried to discuss the fundamental approaches and principles of social protection in Islamic law.

---

30 Ali Fuat Akçapınar, http://www.mirathaber.com/ali-fuat-akcapinar-islam-siyasetinde-bir-sosyal-devlet-modeli-var-midir-22-467y.html (30.01.2018)
31 Kapar, p. 5.

1 Conceptual Framework of Social Protection in Islamic Law

In this part, the definition, importance, purpose, scope, and fundamental principles of social protection in Islamic law will be addressed.

I. The Definition of Social Protection in Islamic Law

Social protection is used today as a new concept that expresses the same meaning as social security and comprises the words "social" and "protection". The word "social" passed from Western languages into Turkish as the provision of the word *içtimaî*, based on the roots of the Arabic language.[32] It expresses as a meaning the matters relating to society and to the various layers of society.[33] In other words, this word, everything regarding humans who live in organized societies or in groups within society, is characterized with the word social. Therefore, any incident must first relate to people before being able to have social characteristics. In this context, all relationships, efforts, and ardor, lifestyle, living standards, and working conditions of people living in regular groups of society or within society are socially thematic constructions.[34] The word "protection" is that which means to guard,[35] in the dictionary, and to prevent things that cause damage, and it is used in the sense of people being able to live without fear, as a provision of the words safety and security.

While social protection is expressed as the objective of social security,[36] it is stated that it is wider and more comprehensive than social security and that

---

32 James Midgley, "Challenges Facing Social Security", *Challenges to Social Security*, Ed.: James Midgley, Martin B. Tracy, Greenwood Publishing Group, Connecticut, 1996, p. 2.

33 Turkish Language Institute Big Turkish Dictionary, http://tdk.gov.tr/index. php?option=com_bts&arama=kelime&guid=TDK.GTS.586a8503dacf31.50664163 (02.01.2017); Mehmet Şeker, *Institutes of Social Solidarity in Islam*, Ministry of Religious Affairs Publications/240, Public Books/76, Ankara 2007, p. 67; Faruk Beşer, *Social Security in Islam*, Seha Neşriyat, Temel Press, Istanbul 1988, p. 59; Murtaza Köse, p. 77.

34 Murtaza Köse, p. 77.

35 Nebi Bozkurt, "Himâye", *Islamic Encyclopedia of Diyanet*, 1998, XVIII/56.

36 Ali Güzel-Ali Rıza Okur, *Social Security Law*, Beta Basım Press, Istanbul 1990, p. 8.

social protection includes special measures that aren't expressly defined in providing social security.[37]

According to Gülmez, who expresses that social protection is the historical, fundamental, and general objective of all social human rights, "Social protection, cannot and should not take the place of the main concept, written as a *right* in in legal documents, of the social state period."[38] Contrary to this, there is also the view that the concepts of social protection and social security can be used[39] synonymously

According to Öztürk, "The concept of social protection, which periodically encounters the concept of social security, expresses the protection of individuals against all kinds of social risk with both the prevention of the emergence of social risks (like educational and health services) and practices directed towards

---

37 A. Bonilla Garcia-J.V. Gruat, *Social Protection- Version 1.0*, International Labour Office, Geneva, 2003, p. 14.

38 "Social security, born from social and economic requirements, is a right that gains its widening, disseminating, and enriching meaning, scope, and content within the process of historical evolution and that is passed to documents. The evolution starting as "social insurance rights" continued with a meaning and content without reference in universal and regional legal documents that, in my opinion, is not accurate, in which social security, which constitutes the general and fundamental objective of all social human rights since the beginning, gained with neoliberal approaches adopted in the globalization years of social protection." (Mesut Gülmez, "Social Security or Social Protection? The "First" Contrarian Thoughts on International Size and Evolution," *Social Human Rights International Symposium*, VII, p. 117) http://www.sosyalhaklar. net/2015/bildiriler/gulmez2.pdf (12.04.2018)

39 "The Board of Directors, which conducted its 294th meeting in 2005, of the International Labor Organization (ILO) discussed a report for the purposes of debate and guidance that synonymously used the concepts of "social protection" and "social security". This document handled social protection or social security within the framework of article 22 of the Universal Declaration of Human Rights, and within the framework of other relevant international working agreements with the Philadelphia Declaration of the Organization and the Minimum Standards Agreement of Social Security No. 102. Based on this, the entirety of the transfers, rights, obligations, measures, organizations, and objectives, which are (i) to eliminate or reduce poverty, (ii) to ensure income assurance to help individuals in overcoming significant risks that life brings (that lead to a loss of income such as unemployment, old age, and failure), and (iii) to guarantee the access of people to health and social services, should be understood from social protection (social security)." (ILO, "Social protection as a productive factor", Governing Body, Committee on Employment and Social Policy (GB.294/ESP/4 294th Session), Geneva, 2005, p. 1; Kapar, p. 3)

eliminating social risk factors (social insurance, individual insurance, social aid, and social service-treatment and rehabilitation, etc.) in the widest sense by also including social security. However, the framework of social security has been drawn up by international social law and accepted as a right; and while it expresses the mechanisms of protection, at a premium or not, that have been institutionalized to prevent the loss of income that more often social risks cause, social protection is accepted as a more open-ended and vague concept compared to social security."[40]

The concept of social security expresses the consideration from the perspective of humanitarian truths of all the occurrences in a social character that are used intensely in the periods following the industrial revolution of the 19th century and that are the subject of the relationships of societal groups and between societies.[41]

Indeed, the concept of social security, used widely in the 20th century, was used primarily in the Social Security Law of 1935 in the United States with the meaning of the term. It was later seen that the concept of social security was used in the 1941 Atlantic Charter, the 1944 Declaration of Philadelphia, and the 1948 Universal Declaration of Human Rights. In today's meaning, it is expressed that the concept of social security gained recognition with the Sir William Beveridge report, completed in 1942, and that the principles of social security laid out in this report had a significant impact on countries understanding of social security.[42]

We should especially point out here that the date on which the term social security began to be used was the end of the 19th and start of the 20th century. However, even if its name isn't social security or social protection, the understanding and tools of social protection rely on the history of humanity. When the understanding of social protection and inception of institutions of social protections in Islamic law become the point in question, this history extends back to the first years of the religion of Islam.[43] Namely, while there is no special definition for the concept of social protection in Islamic law, we see the foundations for this concept in the Medina Islamic State the Prophet Muhammad established

---

40   Şenol Öztürk, "The Approach of New Social Risk in Social Protection," *Social Policy Conferences*, Issue: 66–67 – 2014/1–2, (pp. 43–74), p. 45, footnote no.1. http://dergipark. gov.tr/iusskd

41   Murtaza Köse, p. 77.

42   Mehmet Aykanat, Fundamental Institutions in Ottoman Social Security Law, Selçuk University Institute of Social Sciences, *Unprinted Doctoral Thesis*, Konya 2015, p. 7.

43   H. Ahmet Şimşek, A Sociological Approach to the Institute of Alms in Islam, *Unprinted Graduate Thesis*, Selçuk University Institute of Social Sciences, Konya 1994, p. 5.

as its head of state.[44] Therefore, the emergence and development of social protection in Islamic law came much earlier than the emergence of today's concept of social protection. Modern Islamic legal scholars have examined the concept of social protection and the social protection functions of Islamic institutions in Islamic law after the emergence of the concept.[45] But they see regulations and institutions aimed at social protection in the Islamic legal system not having left needs to social security as the reason for social security emerging much later in the Islamic world than the west.[46]

At this point, there are significant differences in the matters of how societies generally defined social protection and how they approached it. The fact that values, cultures, traditions, institutions, and political structures are different on the national and global scale in turn affects the relationships regarding how social protection is to be provided. It is for this reason that today, just as there is no single definition accepted by everyone, there is not only one approach with regard to social protection.[47] While there have been numerous definitions made for social protection from the past to present, these are some of them:

Social protection means to provide the minimum level of life worthy for a human being, against the various incidences of life, without declining into an extreme state of need, and without sacrificing freedom.[48]

Social protection means the guarantee[49] of protection from the damages of danger that individuals who constitute society suffer beyond their own will, and it is defined as: "a society's mechanism of self-protection through a series of public measures against economic and social risks that may arise for reasons such as disease, birth, occupational injury, occupational disease, incapacity, old

---

44 Ali Fuat Akçapınar, http://www.mirathaber.com/ali-fuat-akcapinar-islam-siyasetinde-bir-sosyal-devlet-modeli-var-midir-22-467y.html (30.01.2018)

45 Aykanat, p. 8. See. Beşer, *Social Security in Islam*, 2016; Hadi Sağlam, "A Summary Analysis of the Historical Roots of Today's Social Security Institution", *Erzincan University Journal of the Institute of Social Sciences (ERZSOSDE)*, IX–I, 2016, 131–142; For detail, see Kâşif Hamdi Okur, *The Example of Surety of Social Responsibility in Islamic Law*, İSAM Publications, 2017.

46 Aykanat, p. 33.

47 A. Bonilla Garcia-J.V. Gruat, p. 14; Ramazan Kılıç; Şahin Çetinkaya, "Social Aid Strategies and a Model Recommendation in the Struggle with Poverty in Turkey", *Dumlupınar University Journal of Social Sciences*, Issue: 34, December 2012, (p. 93–114), p. 95; Kapar, p. 1–2.

48 A. Can Tuncay, *Social Security Law Courses*, Beta Basım Publishing Distribution Co., Istanbul 1984, p. 5.

49 Turan Yazgan, *Turkish Social Security System and Issues (TSGSM)*, Foundation of Research in the Turkish World, Istanbul 1981, p. 7, 8.

age, and death.[50] In this context, social protection means, along with taking the necessary precautions in order to preserve[51] the security of all individuals against income loss and increase that the risks in question, which may arise in society, might cause, the organization or community of organizations[52] that have the duty to preserve economic assurance against a certain number of dangers. In other words, social protection is defined as: "The entirety of institutions that aim to secure the today and tomorrow for the people of a country and that have been established in tight unity between each other." [53]

According to Akyıldız, social protection is much more a social program or system rather than a legal branch that represents the entirety of the rules that guarantee the future of people.[54]

Social protection, especially, is defined as all of the mechanisms that enable the redistribution of income in the foundation of the values of respect for human dignity, social justice, and social solidarity.[55] In this framework, it is necessary both to offer equality of opportunity in reaching societal opportunities without observing any kind of discrimination between the individuals of society and to behave equitably in the distribution of societal opportunities in a manner that will benefit all individuals of society, for the realization of social justice[56,57].

---

50 Yasemin Göknur Ündemir, Forecasting the Important Variables Of Social Security Through Time Series Analysis 2011, *Social Security Expertise Thesis*, Presidency of Turkish Social Security Institution, 2009, p. 3.

51 Okur, p. 290.

52 Nüvit Gerek, A. İlhan Oral, *Social Security Law*, Anadolu University Web-Ofset Publications, Eskişehir 2004, p. 4, 5. https://books.google.com.tr/books?id=Sqkv2o kt95YC&pg=PR1&lpg=PR1&dq=N%C3%BCvit+Gerek,+A.+%C4%B0lhan+Oral+s osyal+G%C3%BCvenlik+Hukuku&source=bl&ots=061l9rRPVR&sig=M9MAbxOB cPloV3Sh-_xTxo2h65A&hl=tr&sa=X&ved=2ahUKEwjehaCY_bzdAhXll4sKHRNF ACoQ6AEwBHoECAYQAQ#v=onepage&q&f=false

53 Hasan Şenocak, "An Evaluation of the Components that Form the Social Security System in Light of the Historical Process", p. 413. 29.12.2017 http://dergipark.ulakbim. gov.tr/iusskd/article/viewFile/1023000094/1023000089 (29.12.2017).

54 Akyıldız, p. 6.

55 Alain Euzeby, "Social Protection: Values to be defended", International Social Security Review, 57, 2/2004, p. 111.

56 In the Holy Quran, it is commanded relating to this matter: "*O you who have believed, be persistently standing firm in justice, witnesses for Allah, even if it be against yourselves or parents and relatives. Whether one is rich or poor, Allah is worthier of both. So, follow not [personal] inclination, lest you not be just. And if you distort [your testimony] or refuse [to give it], then indeed Allah is ever, with what you do, Acquainted.*" (Nisâ, 4/135).

57 Pir Ali Kaya, "*An Evaluation on the Theoretical Framework of Social Justice*", Gift to Prof. Dr. N. Ekin, *Istanbul University Journal of the Faculty of Economics*, p. 229–240.

It is emphasized that a search aimed at eliminating poverty before it emerges is imperative for social protection to be able to be ensured.[58] In this context, the understanding of social protection is discussed in two forms, the narrow and wide sense. Social protection in the narrow sense is the understanding of social protection that ensures security against a certain number of defined risks. In the understanding of social protection in the wide sense takes goals such as the prevention of risks before they emerge and the development of personality.[59]

In this framework, it is stated that the social risks of individuals being secured against economic consequences is within the scope of social protection in the narrow sense. In addition to this, it is predicted that "measures regarding policies of family, housing, urban planning, education, aid in occupational selection, voting power, employment, conjecture, the increase of efficiency, health, and hygiene", are beyond the risks that enter into the scope of social protection in the narrow sense and are in the scope of social protection in the wide sense.[60] Therefore, a social protection limited to economic security of individual is not adequate and it is required to be extended to the development of personalities and talents.

We can therefore say that social protection in Islamic law means the social protection both in the narrow and wide sense. Because all these matters we consider are directly related to the protection of these five universal values of Islamic law (so called *"zarûriyyât-ı hamse"*), which are life, property, intellect, lineage, religion that Islamic law aims to protect.

As a result, we think that social protection, according to Islamic Law, can be defined as the prevention before revelation of risks and dangers and the development of personality for the preservation of these five universal values and as the individual and institutional meeting of all the needs of humans for the protection of these five values.

II The Subject of Social Protection in Islamic Law

As is to be understood from all definitions made regarding social protection, risks/dangers constitute the issue of social protection. The harms humans are exposed to throughout their lives in terms of socioeconomics are called dangers, and a danger being social is because it is a phenomenon that individuals living in society come across. It is expressed that the maintenance of the material of social

---

58 Öztürk, p. 58.
59 Aykanat, p. 8.
60 Okur, p. 291.

risk, meaning people's physical assets, is related only to the elimination of material need. In this context, social risk/danger *is defined as* a situation that, while when it will come about is unknown, is likely and certainly to occur in the future and that leads to a decline in the material assets of individuals exposed to it.[61] In other words, risk/danger means any and all incidents that emerge beyond the willpower of people and constrain the individual from generating income and any and all causes that produce the need for social protection.[62]

Discussing the transformation taking place in the labor market and economic structure together with the effects of the transformation taking place in the societal structure, especially in the emergence of poverty, is seen as necessary for the integral and radical solution in social protection policies today.[63] It is therefore being expressed that the transformations in question taking place in economic, demographic, and societal structures make it necessary to change the understanding of social risk.[64]

Öztürk "emphasized that risks such as being dependent on low-insufficient income for long periods of time; being raised in long-term poverty, low wage-qualified employment, illicit employment, or in frail-defenseless family with a low education level; living in disadvantaged regions or segments of society; or not entering into the labor market because of the obligation for care services or qualitative deficiencies are indicated as the social risks that constitute serious problems in the Social Risks European Union's Social Inclusion Strategy in European Union (EU) nations."[65]

On the other hand, social risks can include different risks and dangers based on the socioeconomic situation and cultural traditions of each country. But an international agreement that specifies the minimum standards regarding these matters and indicates a fundamental standard gained recognition by all social security systems around the world.[66] Along with the International Labor

---

61 Faruk Beşer, Social Risks Insurance and Islam, p. 5. http://sosyalsiyaset.net/documents/sosyal_riskler_sigorta_ve_islam.htm. (12.06.2018)

62 Aykanat, p. 20.

63 Öztürk, p. 47.

64 Öztürk, p. 49. As a matter of fact, the social risk approach or new social risk phenomenon accepted as a new approach in the struggle with exclusion predict that new social protection mechanisms need to be developed by emphasizing that the risk of social exclusion appears in different forms in the new era. It is expressed that the social investment-based social inclusion strategy that the EU adopted with the Lisbon Summit supports this. (Öztürk, p. 59)

65 Öztürk, p. 61.

66 Okur, p. 293.

Organization (ILO) defining the branches of social insurance corresponding to the eight, minimally accepted economic and social risks with the agreement no. 102 in 1952, each country has developed different models of social security based on their own degree of economic development, the economic system they enforce, the status of political conditions, and methods of financing. The nine branches of risk laid out in the 1952 ILO agreement no. 102, to which Turkey is a party, are as follows: workplace accident, occupational illness, disability, old age, disease-health, disease-income, death, motherhood, and unemployment."[67]

In Islamic law, the term "zaruret" is used as a risk/danger that means "large danger and harm in a scale that makes it permissible to violate the prohibitions of the religion of Islam." Because the term distress "encompasses in Islamic law the state of hunger and loss of strength whose compensation will them to difficult harm, if that which someone living in difficulty is exposed progresses and will leave permanent damage."[68]

In this context, "The regulations regarding the preservation of the values that the religion of Islam sees as essential for society and individuals and the benefits these provide with the concept of *zaruriyyât* as the terms fıkıh and usûl-i fıkıh to mean the five fundamental values that constitute the highest degree in the separation of the trio in the form of zarûriyyât-hâciyat-tahsîniyyât of the goals and benefits that the religion observes."[69]

Indeed, in Islamic thought, the matter of the probability of encountering the dangers that always threaten the security of the life and property of humanity is laid out in the Holy Quran like this: "*...And no soul perceives what it will earn tomorrow, and no soul perceives in what land it will die. Indeed, Allah is Knowing and Acquainted.*"[70] In another verse from the Holy Quran, it is proclaimed that, "*Say, "O Allah, Owner of Sovereignty, You give sovereignty to whom You will and You take sovereignty away from whom You will. You honor whom You will and You humble whom You will. In Your hand is [all] good. Indeed, You are over all things competent.*"[71] However, the verse of "*And We will surely test you with something*

---

67 Chapter XI. Ekli Cetvel. http://www.ilo.org/ankara/conventions-ratified-by-turkey/ WCMS_377270/lang--tr/index.htm (25.9.2017); Hadi Sağlam, Religious Officials' Guide to Social Security, Social Security Throughout History, p. 40.15.03.2017
68 For detail, see Halit Çalış, "Zaruret", *Islamic Encyclopedia of Diyanet*, 2013, XLIV/141– 144, p. 142.
69 Mustafa Çağırıcı, "zaruriyyât", *Islamic Encyclopedia of Diyanet*, 2013, XLIV146–148, p. 146.
70 Lokman, 31/34.
71 Âl-i İmrân, 3/26.

of fear and hunger and a loss of wealth and lives and fruits, but give good tidings to the patient" [72] draws attention to the fact that there may be dangers that can threaten the security of the life and property of humans.

It is seen that the Prophet Muhammad drew attention to matters that may be a threat and risk for the reflection of either the individual or society in the hadiths in which he to refuge in God and prayed to God to protect him from these hazards, from the evils of life, from destitution,[73] from helplessness, from famine, from contempt, from inability (from disease and disability), from weakness, from torture and oppression,[74] and from the malice of wealth[75] and poverty.[76]

We should especially note that, according to Islamic law, wealth and poverty are not themselves harm and danger but the unrest and trouble that these may cause are harmful and dangerous. Therefore, it is understood from all these verses and hadiths that people might encounter risks and dangers regarding the five universal values, *zarûriyyât-ı hamse*, that must be protected throughout their lives.

Zarûriyyât expresses the affairs/benefits at the highest level and means the essential, fundamental rights and values for the presence, peace, and order of society.[77] Islamic legal scholars are of the opinion that the provision of the peace and social protection of the individual and society is connected to the preservation of affairs (life, property, lineage, intellect, and religion), referred to with names in the literature like "zarûriyyat-ı hamse", makasıd-ı hamse, külliyyat-ı hams".[78]

---

72 Bakara, 2/155.
73 See Müslim, İbn el-Haccâc el-Kuşeyrî, Sahîhu Müslim, "Zikr", *el-Câmiu's-Sahih*, Çağrı Publications, İstanbul 1981, 60; Ebû Dâvûd, Süleyman b. Eş'as es-Sicistanî, *es- Sünen*, Çağrı Publications, İstanbul 1982, "Edeb", 98; Tirmizî, Muhammed b. İsa b. Serve, *el-Camiu's-Sahih*, Sünenü't-Tirmizî, Egypt 1975, "Da'avât", 61.
74 Ebû Dâvud, "Vitr", 32.
75 See Buhârî, "Da'avât", 39, 44, 46; Müslim, "Zikir", 49; Ebû Dâvûd, "Vitr", 32; Tirmizî, "Da'avât".
76 The negative perspectives of poverty were discussed intensely in the hadiths depicting the truth, and it was taken note what kind of threat and risk there may be for the experience of either the individual or society. (Ahmed b. Hanbel, *el-Müsned*, vol. I–VI, Çağrı Publications, İstanbul 1982, II/231, 250, 410).
77 Hacı Mehmet Günay, "Muhammed Tâhir b. Âşûr'un Makâsıd Anlayışı", Ahmet Yaman, *Intentions and Judicial Opinion, Philosophy of Islamic Law Araştırmaları*, IFAV, 3rd Edition, Istanbul 2017, p. 425; Ertuğrul Boynukalın, "Makâsıdu'ş-Şerîa", *Islamic Encyclopedia of Diyanet*, XXVII, 2003, pp. 423–427, p. 425.
78 See Şatıbî, Ebu İshak İbrahim b. Musa, *el-Muvâfakât fî Usûl'ş-Şerîa*, , Dâru İbn Affân, Saudi Arabia 1997, II/20, 32; İbn Âşûr, Muhammed Tahir, *Makâsıdü'ş-Şerîati'l-İslâmiyye*,

We can say in this context that risks and dangers, which are beyond the control of people and for which it isn't obvious when they will appear, for the life, property, intellect, lineage, and religion of people constitute the subject of social protection in Islamic law.

III The Importance of Social Protection in Islamic Law

Provisions aimed at human's right to life are found in the Torah,[79] Bible,[80] and Holy Quran,[81] which are the sources of all Abrahamic religions. Especially in the Holy Quran, in the verse of: *"... whoever kills a soul unless for a soul or for corruption [done] in the land- it is as if he had slain mankind entirely. And whoever saves one- it is as if he had saved mankind entirely..."*[82] draws attention to the importance of humans' right to life by equating killing one person with killing all people and granting one person the right to live with granting all people the right to live.

In this respect, "the right to life starts from the right of human beings to exist, and thus it emanates from the creation of human beings by God."[83] Therefore, this right granted by God is a leading human right according to Islamic law. The Prophet Muhammad specified the immunity of humans' right to life by proclaiming in an address to all Muslims in his Final sermon that *"However*

Daru'n-Nefâes, Umman (Publication date not available), p. 300; İbn Âşûr, Muhammed Tahir, Philosophy of Islamic Law, The Problem of Intent, Translators: Mehmet Erdoğan, Vecdi Akyüz, Rağbet Publications, Istanbul 2013, p. 225; Ahmet Yaman, "On the Principles of Purposeful Judicial Opinion or Intent/ Theological Interpretation Administration in Terms of Islamic Legal Science", Intent and Judicial Opinion, Philosophy of Islamic Law Araştırmaları, İFAV, 3rd Edition, Istanbul 2017, pp. 161–196; Boynukalın, "Makâsıdu'ş-Şerîa", *IED*, XXVII, p. 425; Adem Yıldırım, "An Overview of the Makasidu'sh-Sharia in Islamic Law Literatüre", *Maslahat in Islamic Sciences*, Editor: Ayten Erol, Gece Kitaplığı Publishing House, Ankara 2017, (pp. 149–172), p. 165–169.

79 See *Scripture/Torah*, Scripture Company, Istanbul 1981, Exit, 20, pp. 13–17; Scripture/ Torah, Tensiye, 5/16–21.

80 See *Scripture /Bible*, Scripture Company ('Together with the Torah, Istanbul 1981), Luka, 18/20.

81 Nisâ, 4/29; Mülk, 67/1–2; Mü'minûn, 23/80.

82 Mâide, 5/32.

83 Osman Taştan, "Human Rights and Religions Education through Islamic Legal Theory", E. Asla, M. Rausch (Eds.) *Religious Education*, Springer Fachmedien Wiesbaden GmbH, Wiesbaden Germany 2018, s. 261.

sacred and innocent are today, this month, and this town, so innocent are your lives, property, and honors.[84]

The Prophet Muhammad drew attention to knowing the value of blessings and taking measures for this and, thus, the importance of social protection by commanding, "*Know the value of the five things, even before the five things: Know the value of living before death, of health before illness, of leisure before occupation, of youth before old age, and of wealth before poverty.*"[85]

And it is for this reason that, according to Islamic law, social protection and the realization of the right to life carry such great importance in terms of meeting the needs of all people for the preservation of the five universal values (life, property, intellect, lineage, religion), which must primarily be protected for life, without regarding their religious, social, or cultural situations.[86]

In this framework, Islamic legal scholars have expressed that all these provisions regarding Islamic law are related to the preservation of the five universal values (makâsıd-ı hamse).[87] The aim from the protection of life for social protection in Islamic law is taking measures against the threats and dangers for the lives of individuals and society. Just like taking measures against infectious diseases, taking protective measures before danger for life yet forms is the necessity for social protection.[88] As no one has the right to take the life that God has given, matters such as unjust homicide,[89] slander,[90] gossip,[91] people killing their

---

84 Buhârî, "Science", 37, "Hajj", 132; Müslim, "Hajj", 147.

85 Aclûnî, İsmâil b. Muhammed, *Keşfu'l-Hafâ*, Beirut, 1351, I/148.

86 http://www.hayrettinkaraman.net/makale/0609.htm. (25.07.2017).

87 Şâtıbî, II/19–20; Cüveynî, Abdülmelik b. Abdullah b. Yusuf, *el-Burhân*, Dâru'l-Kütübi'l-İlmiyye, Beirut-Lebanon 1997, II/79; Gazzâlî, el-Müstesfâ, I/174, 179; Ferhat Koca, "Tûfî", *Islamic Encyclopedia of Diyanet*, 2012, XLI/327–330, p. 328; Ahmet Yaman, "On the Principles of Purposeful Judicial Opinion or Intent/Theological Interpretation Administration in Terms of Islamic Legal Science", *Intentions and Judicial Opinion*, Marmara University Faculty of Divinity Foundation Publications, Istanbul 2017, (pp. 161–196), p. 162; Abdurrahman Haçkalı, "El-İzz b. Abdisselâmda Intent-Judicial Opinion Relationship", (Ahmet Yaman, *in the book of Intent and Judicial Opinion*), Marmara University Faculty of Divinity Foundation Publications, Istanbul 2017, (pp. 285–305), p. 286–287.

88 Hacı Mehmet Günay, "Muhammed Tâhir b. Âşûr'un Makâsıd Anlayışı", Prepared By: Ahmet Yaman, *Intent ve Judicial Opinion, Philosophy of Islamic Law Araştırmaları*, İFAV, 3rd Edition, Istanbul 2017, p. 425.

89 Nisâ, 4/92–93; Mâide, 5/32; En'âm, 6/151; İsrâ, 17/33; Furkân, 25/68.

90 Nur, 24/4, 23–24.

91 Hucurât, 49/12; Hümeze, 104/1–2.

children out of fear of poverty,[92] and suicide[93] have been prohibited. Along with this, is has been deemed permissible to eat harm/banned things in order to save a life. [94]

The religion of Islam has commanded the earning through legitimate means of property in order to protect possessions. It has taken moral and material measures for the protection of property. The unjust earning of goods such as theft,[95] seizure,[96] plunder, bribery,[97] gambling, fraud, cheating, trickery, black market, usury, interest,[98] waste, and the unjust consumption of the property of another[99] have been banned.[100] The obligation of compensation has been brought about for lost and destroyed goods.[101] As it is known, the characteristic that distinguishes humans from other creatures is intellect, and intelligent humans are the interlocutor of religion. Understanding the Book and the Prophets is only possible but with intellect. Therefore, the use of substances such as alcohol and narcotics has been prohibited for the preservation of the intellect,[102] and abstention from evils like hostility, grudges, hate, and jealousy is desired. The religion of Islam has encouraged marriage for the protection of lineage[103] and banned adultery.[104] Religion life, and the protection of religion is the principle. Everybody has the freedom to choose and live out their religion, whether they be

---

92 En'âm, 6/151.
93 The Prophet Muhammad Proclaimed in one of his hadiths, that *"Whoever kills oneself by strangling is to have strangled himself for hell. Whoever is to have beat oneself is to have beaten oneself for hell"* (Buhârî, "Cenâiz", 84).
94 Bakara, 2/173; Mâide, 5/3; En'âm, 6/145.
95 Mâide, 5/38.
96 Bakara, 2/188; Nisâ, 4/29.
97 The Prophet Muhammad proclaimed in one of his hadiths, *"He who gives or takes a bribe is in hell."* (Ebû Dâvûd, "Akdiye", 4)
98 Bakara, 2/275, 278.
99 Bakara, 2/188; Nisa, 4/29, 160–161.
100 The Prophet Muhammad proclaimed in one of his hadiths, *"Whoever steals unjustly the property of another shall later meet the wrath of God."* (Ahmed b. Hanbel, 1/416)
101 Cessâs, *Ahkâmu'l-Kur'ân*, 1, trans.: Muhammed es-Sâdık Kamhâvî, Beirut 1405/1985, p. 326; el-Kurtûbî, *el-Câmi' li Ahkâmi'l-Kur'ân*, (Publisher not available), Egypt 1935/1950, II/357; ez-Zühaylî, Vehbe, *Nazariyyetü'd-Damân ve Ahkâmu'l-Mes'ûliyyeti'l-Medeniyye*, Dımaşk 1402/1982, p. 175.
102 Mâide, 5/9.
103 The Prophet Muhammad announced, *"Whoever among you is strong enough to marry, be married. Because to be married most prevents the eye from straying and preserves chastity and honor."* (Buhârî, "Nikâh", 2)
104 İsrâ, 17/32.

Muslim or not.[105] Indeed, a main reason for the Prophet's request to punish the mischief and corruption is to protect the society and its interests, and therefore for social protection.

When the commands, prohibitions, and recommendations that the religion of Islam has put forth are examined, it is seen that all the provisions are directed towards protecting these values. In Islamic law, the preclusion of all kinds of disorder and conflict that may occur in society is desired with the protection of the values in question, which are valid for both Muslims and non-Muslims alike.[106] According to Islamic law, the preservation of these values is an undeniable right gained from birth. Islamic law has held both the individual and the state responsible for the protection of these fundamental rights that man has brought from birth because he his human.[107] Therefore, these values absolutely must be protected so that these values are not contradicted by all kinds of produced religious information and regulation and so that humans can live as humans.

Social protection is fundamental in the provision of social justice and social peace, according to Islamic law. Social protection, which plays significant roles in the solution of societal problems, constitutes one of the fundamentals of societal and universal peace, because it reduces poverty with the assurance it provides. In the early years of Islam, by commanding in the 1st-3rd verses of the Sūrat al-Māʿūn that: "Did you see he who lies about accounts and the penalty day! He is one who pushes and shoves orphans, who does not support feeding the needy", social cooperation and social protection are emphasized, and the sociopolitical and economic awareness in the Mecca community and that this expresses an evil for humanity are noted. However, those who do not show honor to orphans and who do not encourage the feeding of the poor are negated in the Holy Quran.[108] The command of: *"So as for the orphan, do not oppress [him]. And as for the petitioner, do not repel [him]."*[109] was given, addressed even to the Prophet Muhammad and all Muslims.

---

105 Bakara, 2/256; Kâfirûn, 109/6.
106 Hayreddin Karaman, *Issues of the Day in the Light of Islam 1-2-3*, İz Publishing House, Istanbul 2002, 286; Akyüz, p. 465.
107 İzzet Sargın, The Entirety of Human Rights and the State, *Notices of the Human Rights and Religion Symposium*, 15–17 May 2009, Çanakkale Onsekiz Mart University Publications, Çanakkale 2010, p. 95.
108 See 74. Müddesir, 42–44; 68. Kalem, 24.
109 Duhâ, 93/ 9–10.

In this context, social protection policies and programs based upon social justice, equality, and rights are important in terms of supporting the realization of the human rights of the impoverished, the economically, socially, and politically weak, and the defenseless segments of society.[110]

However, social protection is an inseparable component of social policies observed for the reduction and prevention of poverty in society and contribute as a vehicle to human dignity, equality, and social justice in a degree provided by national solidarity and a fair distribution of burden.[111]

In this framework, and in addition to social protection being a fundamental human right, the provision of social integrity is the foundation in the realization of social inclusion, social peace, and social justice.[112]

The principle found in article 22 of the 1948 Universal Declaration of Human Rights[113] regarding each person having the right to social protection, or in other words, regarding social protection being a fundamental human right, constitutes a universal awareness.[114] In article 25/1 of the same declaration, by saying that "each person has the right to a suitable level of life that provides for health and welfare for either themselves or their families, including food, clothing, residence, medical care, and necessary social services, and the right to security from unemployment, disease, disability, widowhood, old age, and subsistence, in other situations beyond their own will that deprive them",[115] it was indicated that having healthy living conditions and nourishment are fundamental human rights. Article 172 of the Constitution of the Republic of Turkey is directed towards social protection.[116]

---

110 Kapar, p. 6.

111 ILO; *"Report of the Committee on Social Security"*, Sixth item on the agenda: Social security – Issues, challenges and prospects. International Labour Conference, Provisional Record Eighty-ninth Session, Geneva, 2001, p. 33)

112 Kapar, p. 7.

113 "Each person has the right to social security upon becoming a member of society; and the right for indispensable economic, social, and cultural rights to be realized in symmetry with the organizations and resources of the state, by means of national efforts and international cooperation, for their dignity and for the development of their personality." https://www.unicef.org/turkey/udhr/_gi17.html (12.10.2017)

114 Euzeby, p. 109.

115 https://www.unicef.org/turkey/udhr/_gi17.html (12.10.2017)

116 In the 172nd article of the 1982 Constitution directly related to social security: The provision of "The State takes measures that protect and enlighten consumers and encourages the ventures of consumers that are self-protecting" is found. https://www.tbmm.gov.tr/anayasa/anayasa_2011.pdf

In this framework, social protection, by saving individuals and families who have fallen into difficult times, exposed to danger, from the damages of the danger they suffer, is important in terms of ensuring a minimum standard of living,[117] proper for human dignity, within the society in which they live and without needing other people.

Because the protection of these principles is primarily aimed at individuals and society through individuals. In this framework, the ultimate objective of the sending forth of the religion of Islam is to create an unruffled, healthy, and free person who is an absolute owner or material and immaterial responsibility and an orderly, stable, harmonious society that individuals who possess these qualities create.[118]

Proclaiming in the Holy Quran that: *"You are the best nation produced [as an example] for mankind. You enjoin what is right and forbid what is wrong and believe in Allah..."*[119] it was emphasized that the society that bears these characteristics is the most favorable society, to be taken as an example for humankind. Therefore, the moral values of the society which the religion of Islam has set forth will rise up over this widely comprehensive, fundamental principle and will have brought the justice necessary for all of humanity.

Here, the two-way relationship between the realization of one and the existence of the other is in question, and social protection is important both in terms of the general structure of society being orderly and of the situation of each individual that constitutes it being orderly as well.[120]

Social protection presents a level of life fitting the honor of people for all members of society by ensuring the distribution among the members of society of the welfare and wealth coming from economic development. Along with supporting social justice and integrity in this respect, social protection ensures the development of the capabilities of people as well as economic mobility and creativity.[121] Social protection is also important in terms of the development and strengthening of democracy and ensuring political participation.[122]

---

117 Gerek and Oral, *Social Security Law*, Anadolu University, 2004, p. 4.

118 H. Mehmet Günay, The Culture of Poverty as an Element of Risk in the Realization of the Main Objectives of Religion, *Journal of Islamic Legal Research*, Issue: 11, Konya 2008, (pp. 303–316), p. 304.

119 Âl-i İmrân, 3/110.

120 For detail, see Günay, XI/304.

121 Kapar, p. 8.

122 ILO; *"Report of the Committee on Social Security"*, Sixth item on the agenda: Social security–Issues, challenges and prospects International Labour Conference, Provisional Record Eighty-ninth Session, Geneva, 2001, p. 33)

As a result, social protection as envisaged in Islamic law is critical to protect the five key values (life, property, lineage, intellect, and religion) of all humanity from all danger and risks and to sustain them, thus to achieve social justice and peace.

IV The Purpose of Social Protection in Islamic Law

According to the Islamic religion, it is stated in many verses[123] that there is a blessing for those who desire and seek safety and trust. The exigence of the hadith of *"The Believer is someone whom people are sure will not harm life and property"*[124] of the Prophet, known as Muhammedü'l-Emin, draws attention to the qualifications of being trustworthy and reliable, which must be present in all believers.

It was emphasized that the need for the faith of the awareness of security by being proclaimed in another one of the Prophet Muhammad's hadiths, *"Blasphemy, righteousness and deception, infidelity and security cannot be found together in the heart of a person together at the same time."*[125]

Indeed, social protection, defined, according to Sağlam, from the perspective of Islamic law as an umbrella, a shelter, a fortress, a prediction, and a precaution is individual social security, the *"insurance of faith"* in the afterlife, primarily of the individual. Because one meaning of faith is *"security and trust"*. In this context, Sağlam states that, while the trust that all individuals seek out is provided with insurance of faith/trust in the moral space from the individual perspective, it is procured with insurance of social faith/trust from the societal perspective.[126] Therefore, the exertion of a person who believes for not just their own security but for the security of society and humanity is the requirement of faith. We can say in this situation that especially the belief in the afterlife is the greatest assurance for social protection in Islamic law.

In addition to this, it is emphasized in Islamic law that believers are but brothers[127], and the basic aims are highlighted in the provision of safety and trust such as ensuring help and support for the orphans, the poor, and the devoted. In

---

123 Tin, 95/3; Bakara, 2/125; Quraysh, 106/ 3-4; Kasas, 28/57.
124 Tirmizî, "İman", 12.
125 Ahmed b. Hanbel, II/349.
126 Hadi Sağlam, "A Summary Analysis of the Historical Roots of Today's Social Security Institution", *Erzincan University Institute of Social Sciences Dergisi (ERZSOSDE)*, IX–I, pp. 131–142, 2016, p. 132.
127 Hucurat, 49/10.

line with these objectives, Islamic law aims to create a social order that ensures the social development of society and the fulfillment of the duty of people for God, by making dominant the feelings of brotherhood, social solidarity, sharing, and cooperation in society. With this social order aiming to be created, social justice, social peace, and sustainable development will be realized in society.

Along with regulating the education of the individual and societal behaviors for the social protection of the individual and society, Islamic law aims to provide, on the one hand, for the formation of the family and the placement and acting with solidarity of order. On the other hand, it aims for a system of social protection that includes the social cooperation in which the relationships that bind the individual and the state are found and the economic relationships and financial initiatives that establish a reputation for Islamic society.[128]

Along with the causes that lead to the needs of individuals and societies for social protection being universal, they propound a difference for the ways of eliminating these needs. Such that the element of the objective between the system of social protection that Islamic Law provides and the social protection that human legal systems provide are different. The objective in understandings of social protection today are summarized as "The protection of people, for people." According to Islamic law, the objective of social protection is directly related to the justification for the disposition of people.[129] The Holy Quran proclaims as follows with regard to this matter: *"And I did not create the jinn and mankind except to worship Me."*[130] The goal this verse indicates holds that man is not a servant or slave to either his own desires or feelings or to any kind of existence beyond himself, that he allocates his feelings of servitude only to God, and that not only worship such as prayer, fasting, and pilgrimage but all of the life, behaviors, and orientations of man to the extent of the individual and society. Hadith scholars[131] emphasize that, with the answer of the Prophet Muhammad

---

128 Abdullah Nâsıh Ulvân, *The Social Security System in Islam*, Trans.: Nizamettin Saltan, Bakanlar Publishing Ltd. Co., Erzurum 2001, 15–16.

129 Beşer, *Social Security in Islam*, p. 123–124.

130 Zârîyat, 51/56.

131 İbn Ebî Şeybe, Ebû Bekr b. Abdillah b. Muhammed el-Kûfî, *Kitâbu'l-Musannef fil-Ehâdîs ve'l-Âsâr*, vol. I–VII, Riyad, 1409, VII, p. 78; Müslim, "İmân", 1; Taberânî, Ebû'l-Kâsım Süleyman b. Ahmed b. Eyyûb, *el-Mu'cemu'l-Kebîr*, vol. I–XX, Mosul, 1404/1983, XX/175; Gazzâlî, Ebû Hâmid Muhammed b. Muhammed, İhyâu Ulûmi'd-Dîn, (Publisher not available) vol. I–V, Beirut, 1412/1992, IV/576; Taftâzânî, Sa'duddîn Mes'ûd b. Ömer, *Şerhu'l-Ehâdîsi'l-Erba'în li'n-Nevevî*, (together with the Şerhu'l-Ehâdîsi'l-Erba'în belonging to Birgivî and Akkirmânî), Dersaâdet Publications, (publication date and place not available), p. 85; Aynî, Ebû Muhammed Bedruddîn Mahmud

(p.b.u.h.) to the question by the Angel Gabriel of, "What is goodness?" found in
the dialog in the Cibrîl hadith, in the form of: "Your serving as if you are to see
God, because He sees you, even if you do not see Him", each person shall settle
the bill for each of their actions and each word and act is under the watch of God.

Al-Shatibi states that, with reference to the fact that the worldly life is lived for
the afterlife, all Islamic legal provisions have been placed to ensure that people
serve God by keeping them away from sensual pleasures.[132] Therefore, when
all of these are considered, the intentions from "servitude" that are the point in
question, are not just forms of worship (man-God relationships) but servitude is
a wide concept that encompasses all man-man and man-universe relationships.
Therefore, religious strength is influential in areas which law cannot reach.[133]
Because according to the religion of Islam, all religious principles, forms of
worship, social principles, punishments, and legal systems are gathered in the
fact of obedience and submission to God and of transformation of belief in God
into action. This perspective carries the characteristic not just of embodying
man but of the entire universe. As a piece of this universe, man will both gain
the approval of God and melt into the happiness of the world and the afterlife
and will live in complete balance with the other living and non-living beings in
the universe as a social being.[134] Therefore, the objective of social protection,
according to Islamic law, is summarized[135] in the form of "The protection of man
for (the approval of) God. Because religious sanctions are the point in question
of a benefit, not just for a worldly gain but at the same time for the afterlife, in all
work they do for man in accordance with religion, because they observe not only
the world but also the afterlife.[136] Relating to this matter, it is proclaimed in the
Holy Quran: *"No doubt, whoever comes to the Lord as a sinner, there is definitely*

b. Ahmed, *Umdetu'l-Kârî*, vol. I–XI, Matbaa-i Âmire, (publication place not available),
1308, I/334; Kastalânî, Ebû'l-Abbâs Şihâbuddîn Ahmed b. Muhammed, *İrşâdu's-Sârî
li şerhi Sahîhi'l-Buhârî*, vol. I–X, (Muslim side commentary by Nevevî'nin), Beirut,
1305, I/ 140.

132 See Şatıbî, *el-Muvafâkat*, II/63–65.

133 For detail, see Saffet Köse, *Introduction to Islamic Law*, Hikmetevi Publications, Step
Ajans Adv. Publishing Tan Co., Istanbul 2014, p. 43–46.

134 Faruk Yılmaz, *The Economy of Islam and Social Security System*, Compilation: Ömer
Chapra, Hurşid Ahmed, Faruk Yılmaz, Abdurrahman Şah, Turkish-English
Bibliographies: Sabahaddin Zaim, M.N. Sıddiki, Marifet Publications/46, Yaylacık
Press, Istanbul 1991, p. 154.

135 Beşer, *Social Security in Islam*, 1988, p. 124.

136 The Holy Quran proclaims as such with regard to this matter: "And the weighing [of
deeds] that Day will be the truth. So those whose scales are heavy - it is they who will

hell for him. There he shall neither die nor live (a good life). Whoever comes to Him as a believer who has committed good deeds, it is for them there is heaven where he will remain for all eternity, flowing with streams in the highest degrees. You see, this is the reward for those who cleans themselves of sins."[137]

On the other hand, according to Islamic law, a set of moral and material sanctions are in question like, for example, recognizing the right to the poor of the wealth of the rich, with regard to social protection to establish balance between labor and capital. For this reason, Islamic law aims to reduce the differences between the wealth and social strata in society with the other principles and elements that alms, charity, and spoils bring for social protection. With regard to this matter, the verse of *"... so that it will not be a perpetual distribution among the rich from among you"*[138] has drawn attention to the danger of a fortune being able to become a strength that wanders only among the rich. In this case, while the impoverished cannot ensure daily sustenance and most imperative needs, the wealth of the rich can reach great amounts that create danger. Therefore, the objective of social protection in Islamic law is to bring the poor up to the level of the rich whenever possible by limiting the gap between the social strata in society, in order to ensure social justice in society.[139] Because countries develop in the increase at the scale of increase of the incomes of the rich or at the rate that income differences shrink between the rich and the poor.[140]

In this framework, Islamic law takes part in the stages of both formation and division of income pursuant to the principle that wealth not be a strength that wanders in the hands of a class of the rich. In this context, it has created a system of social protection in which social justice is provided with policies like waste,[141] the prohibition of trafficking[142] and interest,[143] alms,[144] and the

---

be the successful. And those whose scales are light - they are the ones who will lose themselves for what injustice they were doing toward Our verses." (A'raf, 7/8, 9)

137 Tâ Hâ, 20/74–76.

138 Haşr, 59/7.

139 Hadi Sağlam, Religious Officials' Guide to Social Security, p. 45. http://kidep.net/wp-content/uploads/din-gorevlileri-rehberi.pdf

140 Ramazan Kılıç; Şahin Çetinkaya, "Social Aid Strategies and a Model Recommendation in the Struggle with Poverty in Turkey", *Dumlupınar University Journal of Social Sciences*, Issue: 34, December 2012, (pp. 93–114), p. 93.

141 (A'râf, 7/31)

142 Kasas, 28/78.

143 Bakara, 2/275–278.

144 Tevbe, 9/60.

encouragement[145] of aid. [146]

According to Islamic law, no matter how dangerous in terms of social peace and social justice the impoverished and needy who cause the fulfillment of the duty of servitude against the Creator are, wealth that exacerbates and dampens social responsibility and sensitivity is just as extreme of a social danger.[147] In the Holy Quran regarding this matter, the exacerbation and deviation of wealth and the damage and destruction it brings to society are mentioned in more than 100 Quranic verses. In these verses,[148] those who possess wealth and richness, demonstrate exorbitance, and are rebellious are explained as bad examples to hold up as an example. It is stated that the wealth of people who spend in abundance but don't know the value of their wealth, who don't aid, who don't give thanks, and who are spoiled and ungrateful will be taken from their hands.[149] However, the fact that the Prophet Muhammad took refuge in God from these shows that they are dangerous.[150] Because in both situations, there is the presence of a psychosocial setting available to make people forget their purpose for creation. And for this reason, both the impoverished must be saved from misery and be generally taken into the scope of social protection and the wealthy must expend a specific proportion of their property and fortune each year to the impoverished to be able to eliminate the bilateral danger and to be able to actualize social justice.[151] Thus, wealth being rasped with the expenditures of social protection and their transfer in the scale necessary are the points in question.[152] In this situation, therefore, a rich Muslim does not have unlimited freedom on matters of spending his own property, according to Islamic law.[153]

On the other hand, the most important objective in the provision of social protection in systems of social protection today is not for those who need social

---

145 Bakara, 2/3, 215, 261, 273; İbrahim, 31; Fatır, 29.

146 Ahmet Tabakoğlu, "Islamic Economics as a Science", *Journal of Islamic Legal Research*, Issue:16, 2010, (s.11–34), p. 11.

147 Beşer, p. 125.

148 See Kehf, 18/34; Mü'minûn, 23/46–47; Sebe, 34/34; Zuhruf, 43/23; Leyl, 92/4; Alak, 96/6–7; Hümeze, 104/2.

149 Kasas, 28/58; İsrâ, 17/16.

150 Buhârî, "Da'avât", 39; Müslim, "zikr", 49.

151 Ali Seyyar, *Social Policy Terminology*, 2nd Edition, Sakarya Bookstore, Adapazarı, 2008; relevant articles. http://www.idefix.com/kitap/sosyal-siyaset-terimleri-ansiklopedik-sozluk-ciltli-ali-seyyar/tanim.asp?sid=V8XK5BH8SS5SHOXTB1CV

152 Beşer, *Social Security in Islam*, p. 124.

153 Hûd, 11/87–88.

protection but for those who meet this need. Yet, social protection is an institution unique to man, and the value of this institution is directly proportional to the value given to people. Understandings of social protection in systems that see people solely as a tool of product are not, as a result, directed towards the provision of human protection but are directed towards the preservation of production.[154] On the contrary, because the source of the provisions relating to the social protection of individuals is, according to Islamic law, based on religion, the aid made to families and individuals of society and individuals having earned the right for this aid is not because it is forced, but originates from people having a reverend[155] existence.[156]

According to the religion of Islam, the biggest honor given to people is to be the caliph of God.[157] Being the caliph to God is to have the authority to judge things on His behalf.[158] Because man is the most honorable of creation, in the most beautiful form in existence (ahsen-i takvim),[159] because he was created to serve God.[160] Man is worthy because he is man. Superiority is with doing good work but with piety.[161]

And it is for these reasons that, even though they are impoverished for the encouragement of the prohibition of mendicity and the implementation of this prohibition, the matter of there being those who do not beg because of their modesty and aid needing to be provided to them is expressed in the Holy Quran as such: *"[Charity is] for the poor who have been restricted for the cause of Allah, unable to move about in the land. An ignorant [person] would think them self-sufficient because of their restraint, but you will know them by their [characteristic] sign. They do not ask people persistently [or at all]. And whatever you spend of good- indeed, Allah is Knowing of it."*[162] As it is seen, this verse expressly reveals the purpose of social protection.

According to Beşer, because man, created to be valuable, honorable, and respectable, opening his hand to other people could mean them defeating this qualification in their eye and the "servitude" changing direction, this is a danger

---

154 Yılmaz, p. 170.
155 İsrâ, 17/70.
156 Yılmaz, p. 157.
157 Bakara, 2/30; En'am, 6/165; Neml, 27/62.
158 Sâd, 38/26.
159 Tin, 95/4.
160 Zâriyât, 51/56.
161 Hucurât, 49/13.
162 Bakara, 2/273.

for the purpose of the existence of man. For this reason, when we consider it in terms of the individual, people may not beg apart from exceptional situations. On the other hand, when we consider in terms of the state tasked with ensuring social protection, man, created "reverently" because they were made to serve God, cannot fall into a state of begging.[163]

As we have previously stated, while the fundamental objective of social protection systems today is "the protection of people, for people", the fundamental objective of social protection in Islamic law is "The protection of man for (the approval of) God". In other words, the protection of those who need to be protected in terms of the five universal values (life, property, intellect, lineage, religion) that must be preserved, by both the individual and the state for the approval of God. However, economic welfare, social justice, equality of opportunity, and cooperation can be ensured for individuals and societies from whom social protection is expected in this fashion.

V The Scope of Social Protection in Islamic Law

Social protection is one of the essential elements of social justice; and social justice can be developed, should all people in society have the economic and social assurances that are the foundation for them to honorably and freely maintain their lives and work. But should the scope and level of protection of the social protection system in society be insufficient, it is a known fact that, rather than guaranteeing social justice, social injustice will proliferate. And it is for these reasons that the change that systems of social protection today are undergoing, together with the insufficiencies regarding the scope, lead to the damage of social justice. For this reason, a sufficient and appropriate social protection must cover all individuals of society against all risks that bring out income precarity, so that social just may occur in society.[164] Because the economic, social, and political benefits expected from social protection are dependent on social protection encompassing all of society and the provision of protection at a suitable level.[165]

In this framework, social protection according to the religion of Islam is propagated so as to encompass all of society starting, especially, from individuals themselves, from families, from the closest surroundings, from

---

163 Beşer, *Social Security in Islam*, 1988, p. 125.
164 Kapar, p. 11.
165 Kapar, p. 10.

neighbors, and from relatives.[166] With regard to this matter, it is proclaimed in the Holy Quran, "...and to parents do good, and to relatives, orphans, the needy, the near neighbor, the neighbor farther away, the companion at your side, the traveler, and those whom your right hands possess..."[167] Bakara sura 177. As it is understood from the verses of: *"Righteousness is not that you turn your faces toward the east or the west, but [true] righteousness is [in] one who believes in Allah, the Last Day, the angels, the Book, and the prophets and gives wealth, in spite of love for it, to relatives, orphans, the needy, the traveler, those who ask [for help], and for freeing slaves; [and who] establishes prayer and gives zakah; [those who] fulfill their promise when they promise..."*, people must try to disseminate this so as to cover the entirety of society, by starting with solidarity and cooperation activities from those closest to them with regard to social protection.

As it is to be seen, the Quran, the first foundational resource of Islamic law, considers the individuals who especially must be protected in terms of social protection and tasks the state with the duty of their protection. In this context, the Quran has explained with the alms verse[168] and other verses[169] the individuals in the scope of protection, especially in terms of social protection.

However, in many verses the disabled and veterans, martyrs, orphans, the impoverished, children, the elderly and even the widows and orphans of wartime and service martyrs are taken under the umbrella of social security. Therefore, according to Islamic law, the state is to use the necessary instruments in providing social protection with the obligatory or arbitrary decision it will make.[170]

According to Kapar, "Social protection encompasses all support of income and service provided by means of income redistribution, in the foundation of the quality of individuals and the rights they have, in the public space, for the purpose of developing living conditions against income precarity and of preventing the regression of levels of living, so that individuals may maintain a life fitting for their pride."[171]

---

166 İsmail Akyüz, , "The Effect of Societal Solidarity of Religious Practices in Islam", *The Journal of Academic Social Science: Studies International Journal of Social Science*, Number 25-I, p. 461-482, Summer I 2014.

167 Nisâ, 4/36.

168 Tevbe, 9/60.

169 Bakara, 2/83, 219–220; İnsan, 76/8; Beled, 90/12–16.

170 Sağlam, Religious Officials' Guide to Social Security, p. 45.

171 Kapar, p. 2.

It is the duty of the government in social protection to help its citizens for at least the provision of the minimum standards of life.[172] Today, directed to provide for this, a social security/protection system as a system formed from *premium/ free or mixed* regimes encompasses public social arrangements, social insurance, social assistance and various social services.[173] *Social insurances*, as a system with premium payments,[174] is processed with the material contribution/premium of the relevant individual, whoever will be receiving the aid; and *social assistance* and *social services* are provided partially or fully from the budget of the state or

---

172 *Encyclopedia of Miracles in Coran and Sunnah "Social Solidarity and Social Security in Islam"* Translated by: Yasmin Muhammed Moslem, www.quran-m.com/firas/en1.

173 Social Aid is a general name given to aid in cash and kind carried out directed towards those in situations of destitution. In this context and being defined as the material support provided as a last resort for individuals who do not have sufficient income, social assistance is defined as any and all material support made for economic and social purposes for individuals or groups in society in situations of poverty or destitution. "It is the entirety of activities and programs carries out by social service experts and other professional members for the purpose of aiding in the development of the state of health and goodness of people, in people becoming more self-sufficient and in the prevention of states of dependence on others, in the strengthening of family connections, and in the successful fulfillment of social functions by individuals, families, groups, or societies."(Kılıç and Çetinkaya, p. 94; Şenocak, p. 409). Sağlam, Religious Officials' Guide to Social Security, p. 13.

174 "Social Insurances: The technique of social security that the industrial revolution revealed. The Industrial Revolution together with economic and demographic developments changed the form of production and the structure of the family, nuclear families took the place of large families as a result of industrialization and urbanization, and these phenomena brought about a vigorous need for social security systems organized at the hand of the state because they made the ways to traditional social security inaccessible. It is for this reason that countries initiated legal regulations in the field of social insurances at the hands of the State. Based on this, "social insurances" established and maintained by the state are deemed permissible as a result of the widespread debates by modern Islamic legal scholars. The premiums that the insured pay in social insurances are perceived as a type of "tax" because they are taken without considering the will of individuals. Even if there are needs and imperatives with time with justifications such as the facts of deductions that are made being mandatory and paid excesses being accepted as the beneficence of the state to its citizen, it has been allowed." (*Tekâfül (What is Islamic Insurance?* http://tekaful.net/?page_ id=148) See for relevant views relating to the issue in Islamic thought. M. Ahmet ez-Zerka, A. Muhammed, Abdülaziz en-Neccâr, *Economics, Banking, and Insurance in Islamic Thought*, Trans.: Hayreddin Karaman, İz Publishing House, Istanbul 2017, pp. 199–272.

by voluntary institutions in society without there being any kind of contribution from the relevant individual.[175] In this context, the formation of social insurances and institutions to provide for social protection originates from the idea of affairs of the state, according to Islamic law.[176]

Because social protection aims to distance individuals from their situations of destitution with understandings of mutual cooperation towards the protection of disadvantaged groups within society, social insurances, social aid, and social services must be utilized in order for an effective social security to be ensured in society. In this case, the provision of income to segments in need whose income has been cut because of any one of the situations of risk within social life, ranging as far as meeting the treatment costs of poor individuals in society, is within the scope of social protection.[177]

It is known that because social protection/security has become a branch within the discipline of social policy by being systemized the system of social protection in Turkey and in some western countries is operated in connection to a Ministry. Social Insurance, the Retirement Fund, and the Social Security Organization for Independent Contractors constitute the social security system in Turkey.

As a result, when it is considered that the social security/protection systems of today have been unable to provide sufficient protection beyond the scope of social protection and against risks,[178] the needy are within the scope of everybody's social protection for the preservation of the five fundamental values (life, property, lineage, intellect, and religion) that are necessary not just to maintain the physical lives of people for the provision of societal justice, equality, and peace, but for society to stay afloat. Thus, the level of an institution to suit human dignity will be able to be provided. We can state that the provision of social protection is in the responsibility of both the individual and the state, according to Islamic law.

VI The Basic Elements of Social Protection in Islamic Law

The understanding of *social cooperation* and *social solidarity* constitute the fundamental principles of social protection in Islamic law. Rather than the term

---

175 Sağlam, Religious Officials' Guide to Social Security, p. 13.

176 Okur, p. 309.

177 Sargın, p. 24

178 Recep Kapar, p. 9.

solidarity, the Arabic concept of *tesânüd*[179] is used as a moral term that expresses the individuals constituting society today living in cooperation with one another and ensuring strength and support for one another.[180]

In Islam, it is a principle that human dignity is protected by society and that people are the ends, not the means, in all kinds of development. In line with this principle, the religion of Islam adopts an understanding of society in which Muslims are together within solidarity and cooperation and wishes for the mobilization of all opportunities for the formation of the foundations of this society for brotherhood, mercy, mutual love and respect.[181] According to Islamic law, arrangements for social protection and social solidarity rely on the words and spirits of the masses (Holy Quran and Sunnah).

With regard to this matter, numerous provisions are found in the Holy Quran[182] and the hadiths[183], including those related to both individual and communal cooperation. For example, it is proclaimed in the Holy Quran, *"...And cooperate in righteousness and piety, but do not cooperate in sin and aggression..."*[184] and *"They ask you, [O Muhammad], what they should spend. Say, "Whatever you spend of good is [to be] for parents and relatives and orphans and the needy and the traveler. And whatever you do of good - indeed, Allah is Knowing of it."*[185] In addition to this, the Prophet Muhammad proclaimed, *"Whoever alleviates a*

---

179 The term Tesânüd, in the dictionary, means *to rely, lean*, and arises from the root *sened*. (İbn Manzur, Cemalüddîn Muhammed b. Mukrem, *Lisânü'l-Arab*, Dâru Sadr, Beyrut, (publication date not available), "snd" md.)

180 "Concepts, such as *teâvün* (cooperation), *tezâhür* (mutual support), *tenâsur* (cooperation), *tedâmün* (supporting one another), *teâlüf* (commingling), *teâhî* (forming brotherhood), *tevâsül* (establishing relationships with one another) with the same or relative meanings are present in the resources. In Modern Arabic, *tekâfül* is used more commonly rather than *tesânüd*." See for gen. info. Osman Demir, "tesânüd", *Islamic Encyclopedia of Diyanet*, 2011, IL/526–527.

181 Akyüz, p. 472.

182 Al-i İmran, 3/92; Zariyât, 51/19; Nahl, 16/90; Haşr, 59/9; Münafikun, 63/10–11.

183 According to as is was related by Ebû Hüreyre, the Prophet Muhammad proclaimed like this: *"Benevolence is necessary each day for each joint of people. Your ruling with justice between two people is benevolence. Your helping he who wishes to mount his saddle or your loading his burden upon his saddle is benevolence. Words of wisdom are benevolence. Each step you take while going to the mosque to pray is benevolence. It is also alms for you to remove from the road that which causes passersby trouble."* (Buhârî, "Mezâlim", 3; Müslim, "Birr", 58.

184 Mâide, 5/2.

185 Bakara, 2/215.

worldly distress from a believer, God in turn shall alleviate a distress of that believer on the day of judgement. Whoever provides ease to one fallen upon hard times, God in turn shall provide ease in the world and in the afterlife. Whoever covers the shame of a Muslim, God in turn shall cover his shame in the world and in the afterlife. As long as a believing servant aids his religious brothers, God in turn shall aid him..."[186] The Prophet Muhammad proclaimed in the lines of one of his hadiths that, *"To give charity is the duty of all Muslims."* What if he who will give alms cannot find anything? they said. He proclaimed, *"He shall engage in manual labor, which shall be both beneficial unto himself and considered charity."* What if he is unable (or cannot find work)? they asked. *"He shall aid those who have fallen on hard times, on those in need,"* he proclaimed. What if he is unable to do this? they asked. *"He would recommend doing good works,"* he stated. And if he can't do this? they said. *"He shall distance himself from doing evil. This too is considered alms for him,"* he proclaimed.[187] Therefore, as it is to be understood from either the verse or the hadiths, cooperation and solidarity are designed on the subjects of goodness and piousness. Cooperation cannot be the point in question in situations of evil and hostility.

In this case, social solidarity in Islamic law brings together all the responsibilities of individuals that constitute society in the society in which each of them lives. The responsibility in question is in a scale at which everyone, from the simplest individual to the highest administrator of society, will be able to do their part. In social solidarity, the feeling that each individual in society has a set of duties and responsibilities that they must fulfill for themselves and for society is gained. The understanding settles that there is a set of rights of individuals and society against one another with this feeling. Individuals who act with this understanding avoid irresponsible behaviors such as negligence and disinterest while fulfilling their duties and responsibilities.[188] Therefore, we are of the opinion that the five universal principles that must be protected in Islamic law, whether rich or poor, must be in the scope of the social protection of all humans who have needs regarding their preservation.

In this context and according to Islamic law, in covering the needs of the individual in the field of social protection and in the provision of sustenance, all social segments, groups, and the state, respectively, are held responsible, starting

---

186 Müslim, "Zikr", 38. Also see. İbni Mâce, "Mukaddime", 17.

187 Buhârî, "Zekât", 30, "Edeb", 33; Müslim, "Zekât", 5.

188 Mehmet Şeker, *Institutes of Social Solidarity in Islam*, Ministry of Religious Affairs Publications, Ankara 2007, p. 73.

primarily with the individual and later their family and close relatives.[189] In other words, whenever a social problem is encountered, the most primary responsibility at the point of resolution resides with the individual. Should a person be unable to overcome these problems by themselves, their family, relatives, neighbors, and friends (private sector) should step in. Should this also be insufficient, religious institutions and benefactors should be tasked with solving these problems. Should all of these routes be insufficient, the responsibility of the state should begin in providing social welfare and social protection.[190]

The Holy Quran proclaims as follows regarding this matter: *"Does man think that he will be left neglected?"*[191] and *"Then you will surely be asked that Day about pleasure."*[192] The Prophet Muhammad indicates the responsibility to observe and protect by proclaiming that: *"All of you are shepherds, and all of you are responsible for that which you herd. The head of state is a shepherd and is responsible for those over whom he watches (citizens). The head of the family is the shepherd within the family and is responsible for those over whom he watches and for the household. The servant is a shepherd with regard to his master's property and is responsible for that over which he watches." "Man is a shepherd with regard to the property of his father and is responsible for that over which he watches. In sum, all of you are shepherds and are responsible for that over which you watch."*[193]

Because volunteerism is a principle in cooperation and solidarity, which are the fundamental elements of social protection in Islamic law, the difference of religion doesn't even remove this obligation of relatives, according to Hanafi legal scholars. However, should relatives not have enough strength for this, the duty to support those in need falls to the society. Sometimes, society brings this duty to the place of the state. If the state neglects its duty, whoever is in a state of need has the right to initiate legal action by means of judgement.[194] This also shows that providing assistance to those in need is primarily the duty of the

189 Demir, p. 526; Hadi Sağlam, Social Security Institutions and Techniques of Social Cooperation and Solidarity in Islamic Legal History, p. 8.

190 Sağlam, , "Social Security Institutions and Techniques of Social Cooperation and Solidarity in Islamic Legal History", p. 102. http://eski.bingol.edu.tr/media/154992/dddtamami.pdf

191 Kıyame, 75/36.

192 Tekâsür, 102/8.

193 Buhâri, I/215, "Cuma", 11; II/79, "Cenâiz", 33; III/87–88, "İstikraz", 20; VIII/104, "Ahkâm", 1; Müslim, "İmâret", 20; Ebu Dâvûd, "İmâret", 1-13.

194 Demir, p. 527.

relatives in cooperation and solidarity in Islamic law, and that to us, everyone carries responsibility in their own way and that nobody is without responsibility.

Çalış takes notice of the matter that the most effective way to secure the rights here is the value of belief in individuals and the sense of mission formed in the framework of the sensibility of accounting. We believe that Çalış' view that this understanding loads responsibility and duty on all members of society and, at the same time, specifies everybody in society as the defender and auditor of rights and justice[195] is well-directed.

At this point, it is essential that each individual is primarily self-sufficient in the social protection of families and society, and this is accepted as a form of worship according to Islamic Law. The state, along with preparing opportunities for this, opens up opportunities for employment. Begging and the burdening of others was attempted to be prevented through legal, moral, and religious sanctions. But despite everything, the person who is unable to be self-sufficient is referred by the state first to their relatives. Thus, along with relatives being forced to encourage each other to work having been ensured, caring for those who truly need to be supervised is to have been made easier before the law with feelings of kinship and religion. Whether the financial transfers that must be made in this way to those in need go to those who are not in need is to have been brought under control However, those without the opportunity of social protection by their relatives are in the patronage of society - the wealthy - with the guardianship of the state. All humanitarian needs are met in such a way as to legally produce the right to request. There are no conditions for this such as working a specific business day, having invested a certain premium, adhering to a specific social security institution, even to be of this or that religion, or to be exposed to this or that risk.[196]

In this framework, Islamic Law tasked both the state and the individuals with ensuring social protection and asked all individuals in society to run to the aid of the impoverished, primarily families. Thus, even if the state takes no measure, people must willingly help those in need.[197]

---

195 Halit Çalış, "Islam and Human Rights: The Duty-Prioritized Model of Society", *Notices of the Human Rights and Religion Symposium*, 15–17 May 2009, Çanakkale Onsekiz Mart University Publications, Çanakkale 2010, p. 81.

196 Faruk Beşer, *Women's Studies and Social Security in Islam*, Nûn Publishing House, Kilim Press, Istanbul 2009, p. 170.

197 Servet Armağan, "Basic Institutions of Social Security in the Religion of Islam", *Journal of Islamic Legal Research*, iss. 14, Dumat Ofset Publishing Co., Ankara 2009, p. 83.

Islamic law, whether Muslim or not, is always on the side of the oppressed. Just like wealth is not only a reason to give thanks, poverty is not only a reason for trial. Mostly looking out for the impoverished is desired for the social protection of the individual and of society. With regard to this matter, it is proclaimed as such in the Holy Quran: *"They ask you, [O Muhammad], what they should spend. Say, "Whatever you spend of good is [to be] for parents and relatives and orphans and the needy and the traveler. And whatever you do of good - indeed, Allah is Knowing of it.""*[198]

"The giving hand is above the taking hand"[199] is held in the hadiths relating to our topic. Nevertheless, by the truth of society not being ignored, and by means of commanding that *"It is not us who lies full while our neighbor is hungry",*[200] social protection is emphasized by being reminded that the impoverished segments of society must not be forgotten. Social cooperation and solidarity in the area of social protection are highlighted, by commanding in the other hadiths relating to this that: *"One cannot have faith in God as long as he does not ask for his fellow believe that which he asks for himself",*[201] *"Muslims are like the organs of a body in loving and hurting one another. If one organ complains, the other organs of the body join in the pain and run to its aid",*[202] *"The believer is like a building, which is the support that connects the parts to one another, against the believer."*[203]

Social solidarity, as the most fundamental principle of social protection, expresses the integrity of the instruments that ensure the redistribution of income for protect and develop levels of living of people who encounter risks like *old age, disability, illness, birth, death,* and *unemployment.*[204]

One of the methods of social protection that remains outside of the treatment and insurance fulfilled by the state is social aid. Social protection aid directed towards the provision of social protection to disadvantaged groups should be made of sufficient income support to impoverished or needy individuals until they have entirely corrected their conditions of poverty and have become able to meet their own basic needs without requiring assistance.[205] A prevailing

---

198 Bakara, 2/177, 215.
199 Buhârî, "zekât", 18; Müslim, "zekât", 97.
200 Suyutî, Abdurrahmân b. Ebî Bekr, *el-Camiu's-Sağir*, Dımeşk, 1986, II/228.
201 Buhârî, "İman", 7.
202 Buhârî, "Birr", 37; Müslim, "Birr", 66.
203 Buhârî, "Edeb", 36.
204 Sağlam, Religious Officials' Guide to Social Security, p. 13.
205 Ebru Sargın, p. 21.

measure of Islamic law is that "right hand giving aid should not felt with the left one"[206]

We should especially note here that in the understanding of social aid, it is important for the social aid of needy individuals to be perceived as a temporary solution. For this reason, social assistance must be in amounts that will encourage employment for the disadvantaged groups benefitting from social assistance. Otherwise, if social assistance that aims to eliminate individuals' states of need can be carried out within a structure that creates dependency, they can make people lazy. For this, systems of social aid must be operated in relation to institutions of employment.[207] In other words, according to Islamic law, the basic principle in the social protection of society should be to help the impoverished so as to protect their respectability within society and to bring these people into states of productivity and societal benefit by providing work to those able to work, and the provided aid should not break their desire to work.

If this is so, then we can say that the right of social protection as a command of the Holy Quran[208] is a right existing in Islamic law for the impoverished, weak, and outcast, and people are under the guarantee of social protection without considering whether they are Muslim or not. Ömer provides as an example for this topic the salary system paid from the treasury of the Islamic state by means of the council formed at the time.[209]

In the scope of social protection in Islamic law, the elimination through a means appropriate for human dignity of the dangers and risks directed at the preservation of especially the five universal values (zarûriyyât-ı hamse) and the

---

206 http://www.yenisafak.com/yazarlar/hayrettinkaraman/yoksullara-yardim-nasil yapilmalidir-15681.

207 Ebru Sargın, p. 22.

208 *"Righteousness is not that you turn your faces toward the east or the west, but [true] righteousness is [in] one who believes in Allah, the Last Day, the angels, the Book, and the prophets and gives wealth, in spite of love for it, to relatives, orphans, the needy, the traveler, those who ask [for help], and for freeing slaves; [and who] establishes prayer and gives zakah; [those who] fulfill their promise when they promise; and [those who] are patient in poverty and hardship and during battle. Those are the ones who have been true, and it is those who are the righteous."* (Bakara, 2/177).

209 İbn Haldûn, Abdurrahman, *Mukaddime*, vol. I–III, Kahire 1401, II/ 676; Mustafa Fayda, "Fey", *Islamic Encyclopedia of Diyanet*, 1995, XII/ 511–513, p. 513; Hadi Sağlam, *Social Security Institutions and Techniques of Social Cooperation and Solidarity in Islamic Legal History*, 8. http://www.e-akademi.org/incele.asp? 1242645203&url=makaleler/ hsaglam-2.htm. For detail, See Abdülazîz ed-Dûrî, "Divan", *Islamic Encyclopedia of Diyanet*, Istanbul 1994, IX/ 377–381, p. 378.

integration and institutionalization of responsibility are a need by disseminating individual responsibility all throughout society.[210] According to Islamic law, the elimination of this need and the ability to provide social solidarity and cooperation in society are realized by the regulations, institutions, and instruments of social protection, being *mandatory* and *voluntary*.

Islamic law introduces numerous regulations/institutions/instruments of imperative social protection to directly or indirectly transfer the material resources to those in need and thus to accomplish social protection. Most important ones are *the principle of brotherhood,*[211] *the institution of family, the state (beytülmâl), reparations*[212] *and retribution,*[213] *alms,*[214] *and*

---

210 Sağlam, "Are Reparations in Islamic Legal History the Insurance of Today?", p. 292; Okur, p. 325.

211 "If you see the believers just like a body in loving one another, being compassionate to one another, and being charitable to one another; (meaning) if one member falls ill, the other members restlessly and passionately join together against their illness." (Buhârî, VII/77–78, "Edep", 27)

212 Reparations, as an Islamic penal law term, means the payment of a fee from the assets of the perpetrator that must be paid because of deliberately murdering someone or intentional homicide perpetrated against an organ. For relevant verses, see En'am, 6/164; İsrâ, 170/15; Fâtır, 35/18; Zümer, 39/7; Necm, 53/38.

213 "Kasâme: 'Should an unsolved murder be committed in a space open to the public or on private property and should those close to the deceased proceed by legal means, a certain number of people from the community of where the murder was committed must be made to sweat that they did not commit the murder and that they do not know the perpetrator; and following this vow, if the murder was committed on private property, then the owner of that private property shall be made to pay the fee of the murdered individual; and if it was committed on a space open to the public, then the community of that place shall be made to pay. The think targeted with this method is the sharing of responsibility that emerges as a result of a crime. Responsibilities in Islamic law are specified in accordance with mechanisms of reprisal and reparation, and crimes of homicide normally punished with retaliation are punished with reparation should the perpetrator be unknown. The debt of reparation that emerges in the institution of kasâme is paid by the community of where the body was found. The members of the community in question are considered to have minimally disturbed the peace because they were unable to prevent such an incident from occurring within their own living spaces and because they were unable to see or capture the murderer; and they are left to pay the reparations for the murdered individual. Therefore, a crime perpetrated by a single individual is subjected to a collective sanction. Eren Paydaş, "The Institution of Kasâme in Terms of Sociology of the Law", *Marmara University Faculty of Law Journal of Legal Research*, 21, (pp. 595–614), p. 597.

214 Tevbe,9/60.

charity,[215] *along with sacrifice,* [216] *wills, reprisal, ransom, fines of malice paid in provision to banned actions committed during the haj, alimony,* [217] *offerings,* [218] *penances,* [219]*and aid provided to the impoverished by the state treasury.* Such that material penalties even having been brought in response to a number of deficiencies made on the subject of worship is related and the protection of the poor is directly related to the provision of social protection.[220]

In addition, there are nonobligatory social protection institutions that are left entirely to the wishes and desires of people, *futile charity*[221] *and alms, foundations,* [222] *indentured alms, wills, feasts, loans of belongings,*[223] *altruism,*[224] *gifts, grants, vicinity rights, and benevolent loans*[225] in Islamic Law, which accomplish the social

---

215 Bakara, 2/184.
216 Kevser, 108/ 2.
217 The purpose of alimony is the assistance ordered to be made from the rich to the poor among close relatives. (Bakara 2/232; Nisa, 4/ 63)
218 Bakara, 2/270; Hac, 22 /30.
219 Penances are the point in question in situations relating to accidental homicide, intentionally breaking fast during Ramadan, and oaths. Bakara, 2/222; Maide, 5/89.
220 For detail, see Şeker, pp. 134–186; Sağlam, The Institutions of Social Security and Techniques of Social Cooperation and Solidarity in Islamic Legal History, p. 6; Armağan, pp. 69–71; Karaman, The Issues of Today in the Light of Islam, I.
221 Bakara, 2/196, 263, Nisâ, 4/114, Tevbe, 9/103, Mücâdele, 58/12.
222 Foundation is to give an owned asset as alms to the benefit of the impoverished or by other charitable means, remaining within the property of one who consecrates. "It provides important contributions to society as an institution of cooperation that relies on Islamic law and shows itself in different forms within the historical process. Donated assets leave the property of one who is donating and become the property of society. Such management of assets is according to the conditions and general principles in the charter of the foundation." (Yusuf Şen, "An Evaluation on the Social Dimension of Foundations in Islamic Law", Journal of Islamic Legal Research, Issue: 17, 2011, (pp. 415–426), p. 415). For detail, see Şeker, pp. 187–232; Armağan, pp. 72–77.
223 A gratuitous loan as an agreement is to provide for the cost-free use of an asset to another person.
224 Altruism, to prefer another to one's own pleasure, may a coming benefit come across not me but another one of my believing brothers. (Karaman, The Issues of Today in the Light of Islam, I).
       For detail, see Şeker, pp. 187–232; Armağan, pp. 72–77. to say and act according to this. For the relevant verse, see Haşr, 59/9.
225 A benevolent loan (karz-ı hasen) is a legal term that means the interest-free borrowing of money. With regard to this matter, it is proclaimed in the Holy Quran: meaning, "Whoever gives a beautiful loan (without expecting compensation) to God, God shall

protection and solidarity. However, it was noted that, should the arrangements in this second group of the elderly be fulfilled, the relevant people and institutions will gain merit. [226]

Indeed, it is seen that the arrangements and institutions in the history of Islamic law that have functions of solidarity and cooperation that would ensure social protection in society were implemented, placed, and developed after the establishment of the first Islamic state in Medina.[227] Especially assistance made for Ashab al-Suffa, brotherhood formed between ansars and immigrants, and first examples of foundational institutions have become the arrangements and institutions that bring forth social solidarity. Institutions of reparation and retribution are examples of intracommunity solidarity. In this framework, the institution of reparations comes across a legal assurance, being regulated by the State in the Constitution of Medina. In addition to this, shares were allocated to those in need from the captures, alms were collected at the hand of the state and distributed to those in need, and social protection was ensured by implementing the benevolent loan institution in the form of an official institution.[228]

At this point, one of the mandatory organizations of social protection institutionalized as a means/technique of solidarity and cooperation against dangers and risks in Islamic law is the "system of reparations". This system doesn't just leave the guilty to pay the reparations of the victim but brings the responsibility to pay to their close relatives. The system of reparations, which gradually developed as of the era of the Râşit Caliphs, transformed into a joint institution of solidarity and cooperation among certain branches of business and members of professional groups. Therefore, the reason for its provision in the institution of reparations is mutual cooperation and solidarity, and for its philosophy is the lightening of risk by distributing reparations among society. It is stated that this institution, being removed from the scope of inter-family and inter-clan, leaves its place to the cooperation between certain lines of business like drivers, teachers, and doctors and members of the same professional groups because of societal change and development.[229] However, in the structure of the system of

---

pay this back many times more. He who is limited or widened is God, and you will be made to turn unto Him" (Bakara, 2/245; Hadîd, 57/11).

226 Armağan, p. 68. For detail, see pp. 78–82.

227 Hayreddin Karaman, *Islamic Legal History*, İz Publishing, Istanbul 1999, p. 79, 87; Aykanat, p. 33.

228 Aykanat, p. 28; Hadi Sağlam, Religious Officials Guide to Social Security, p. 13.

229 Sağlam, "Are Reparations in Islamic Legal History the Insurance of Today?", p. 271. Also see. Beşer, Social risk-danger, p. 50.

reparations, important changes occur as a result of social phenomena, scientific developments, economic conditions, and commercial practices.[230]

Indeed, the system in Islamic law of reparations, whose name is not widely known even today, is a system that compensates for loss and protects the value of humans in incidents of mostly injury and murder, including workplace accidents, on the one hand and has a multifaceted character, such as providing the maximum precaution and minimal loss with the auto-control feature in its structure in these types of incidents on the other hand.[231]

According to Islamic law, the *institution of the family*, which provides for social solidarity and cooperation in society, is among the mandatory institutions of social protection. Because the family is the protector of the religious, national, and cultural identity, of the human values, and of historical continuity in society, and it is an institution that is universal and has no alternative, in which the personality of the individual is constructed as a transponder. Many verses in the Holy Quran[232] and the hadiths we stated above with regard to social cooperation and development are constituted based on this matter. All kinds of risk and damage that family members encounter directed at the zarûriyyât-ı hamse (life, property, religion, intellect, lineage) can be eliminated or reduced by the other members of the family in Islamic law. The family is a very important institution of solidarity and cooperation in terms of "the protection of lineage", one of the five universal values that must be protected in Islamic law of the protection of family values for its continuation, of rearing children and youth as beneficial members of society, and of being the most important solution address in overcoming society's fundamental problems.

Today, it is known that the economic social, and cultural rights that are necessary for the ability to provide the development of human dignity and personality and social protection are being attempted to be fulfilled thanks to national efforts and international collaboration, considering the resources of each country. In this context, the preservation and strengthening of the family is found in the foundation of social policy both in our country and around the world, directed towards the provision of social protection, and studies are being conducted in this framework. For example, the World Family Organization (WFO), a subsidiary

---

230 Sağlam, "Are Reparations in Islamic Legal History the Insurance of Today?", p. 289; For detail, see Kâşif Hamdi Okur, *The Example of Social Responsibility Surety in Islamic Law*, Center for Islamic Studies (İSAM) Publications, Istanbul 2017.

231 Beşer, Social Security in Islam, 1988, p. 256.

232 Nahl, 16/90; Bakara, 2/177, 215; Nisâ, 4/36.

of the United Nations (UN), has been organizing the World Family Summits with a body of participants comprising national governments, ministries, local authorities, NGOs, parliaments, academics, the private sector, media, and families from various countries around the world since 2004.[233] In this framework, what was taken on a global scale at the summit organized in the United Arab Emirates - Abu Dhabi (World Family Summit+7) December 5–7, 2011 can be summarized as follows:

- "Countries, governments, parliaments, judicial systems, the private sector, and civil society organizations should continue by increasing their current studies for sustainable development. Work that suits social protection and human dignity is valid for all family members. Social protection should be supported with educational programs for children and youths.
- It should be supported primarily with measures of universal social protection.
- Work opportunities to suit people should be sustainable.
- Suitable conditions should be created for women and men in addition to the youths who will be joining the workforce.
- Governments should support social protection programs.
- They should provide contributions of equality everywhere, for social protection and peace. Tolerance for this is important in families, societies, villages, cities, the world, everywhere. Because tolerance is the sharing of equality.
- Strengthening women is very important to decrease poverty in societies and cultures all over the world and to increase the welfare of families.
- A central, international law should be developed and implemented around the world to ensure equality and prevent injustice on the subject of women, children, and families.
- For the struggle against poverty and social exclusion, participation in employment and access to all resources, rights, goods, and services must be made easier. Additionally, the risks that social exclusion brings should be prevented, those who are in positions of weakness and vulnerability should be aided, and all relevant organs should be put into effect.
- The opportunities for work must be increased for families.
- Women and men should be guaranteed to attain reasonable and productive work in free and equal conditions.

---

233 For detail, see Ayten Erol, "World Family Summits", Activity Evaluation, *Kırıkkale University Journal of the Faculty of Islamic Sciences (KİİFAD)*, c. 1, Issue: 1, 2016, p. 75–82.

- Harmful child labor should be eliminated and children should be encouraged to go to school.
- In order to guarantee the futures of families, the provision of youth employment and the transition from school to work should be well administered.
- Academic and political measures must be taken in the prevention of violence.
- With programs of education and instruction, feelings of violence in people, in families, and in society can be taken under control.
- On the subject of education (especially for that of girls) sensitivity and awareness should continue to be created.
- Media should be a positive role model at the point of preventing violence against children and preserving family values.
- The process of peace affects social justice. Political stability is very important.
- Opportunities should be created to create employment, investment, entrepreneurship, skilled development, business, and sustainable livelihood.
- In order to encourage productivity by ensuring safe working conditions for men-women, sufficient leisure time and rest, time off, caring for family and social values, providing adequate compensation in cases of lost or diminished income, and access to sufficient health services should be allowed.
- Workplace rights must be guaranteed, worker's rights must be guaranteed, and there must be workplace laws for all employees and especially for disadvantaged and impoverished workers for their representation, participation, and own interests.
- Governments, employers, workers and productive employment, and work that suits human dignity should harmonize internationally among civil societies that are key factors for the provision of a just globalization, the decrease of poverty, justice, and inclusive and sustainable development.
- The current systems of social protection must be strengthened; and sufficient social protection for all people, guaranteed public employment for disadvantaged groups, income assurance, and health services must be provided.
- In order to be able to employ those who remain unemployed for a long period of time, participation in the labor force market must be ensured by means of developing skills."[234]

The dangers that people come face-to-face with today are different today against new technological developments, and thus the tools used in the provision of social protection in society are diversifying and taking shape.[235]

---

234 Erol, "World Family Summits", pp. 79–82.
235 Hadi Sağlam, Religious Officials Guide to Social Security, p. 45.

Despite this, we believe that the idea that the abandonment and non-implementation of arrangements and institutions for social protection in Islamic law in Muslim societies today is seen as a reason for the increase in the need for social protection[236] is well-directed. Because social protection institutions/regulations/instruments in Islamic law for the provision of social justice and social protection in society have more opportunities for financing from amounts that social protection institutes today obtain in the prevention of socioeconomic dangers. In this context, the aspects of danger don't quite matter, because the phenomena seen today as danger are most of the time seen as a blessing with different aspects, according to Islamic law, and its precautions are taken without revealing these. Therefore, arrangements and institutions for social protection in Islamic law, particularly alms, each operate as a sensitive organizer in Islamic society, and as a result of material transfers between the rich and poor, social justice is attained without even realizing it.[237] For example, in the two-and-a-half year caliphate period of the Emevi caliph Ömer b. Abdülaziz, this problem was resolved on Islamic lands and even no impoverished people were found to give alms to.[238] Therefore, when only alms are considered, it is an important institution in and of itself for the social protection of society. Because alms are not from income but are an amount taken from wealth such that it constitutes a very large fund. Because the areas in which spending is to occur are expressly indicated in the Holy Quran[239], alms cannot be used in general state expenses.[240]

Naseh Ulwan is quoted *"it is obvious that when the principle of Zakat used to be applied in previous Islamic eras, it succeeded in combating poverty, enhancing social solidarity, beating envy and grudge felt by the poor towards the rich, ... making believers accustomed to generosity and donation, and paving the way for the broke to find jobs"*. Thus, zakat was not just giving money to feed the poor, but also it was a means for beating poverty through providing additional access to employment opportunities. For example, a poor young man can be given a capital of a business with which he can buy a machine for

236 Abdullatif Al-i Mahmud, *et-Te'min el-İctimaî fi Dav'iş-Şeriati'l-İslâmiyye*, Dârü'n-Nefais, Beirut, 1994, p. 119.
237 Beşer, Social Security in Islam, 1988, p. 256.
238 See İsmail Yiğit, "Ömer b. Abdülazîz", *Islamic Encyclopedia of Diyanet*, Istanbul 2007, XXXIV/53-54, p. 54.
239 Tevbe, 9/60.
240 Yılmaz, p. 185.

a craft at which he is skillful. So, zakat is a means of development and actual beating of poverty. [241]

This situation shows that alms have an important function that serves social peace and that strengthens solidarity among the different segments of society. Because the degradation of income distribution is a phenomenon that threatens societal peace because wealth gathers in the hands of few. The religion of Islam prohibits meeting the needs of those in economic need with loan interest and substitutes unrequited alms in place of this. No doubt those who have greater economic strength than need giving unrequited financial support to those in need will contribute to economic stamina and therefore to social protection.[242]

In addition, one possible placement of zakat is particularly to indebted people. Any social protection institution financial supporting the indebted is yet known. In the same manner, provisions regarding interest[243] indirectly ensure the preservation of debts and aim to prevent them from becoming poor by losing their economic freedoms under the burden of interest.[244] For this reason, according to Beşer, we can state that we agree with the opinion that there is no social protection in an institutional sense today and that there are social institutions/arrangements/instruments that do allow for insecurity and danger.[245]

"Aid, alms, and benevolent loans"[246], as the regulation/mediation of voluntary social protection in Islamic law, are the three forms of aid and solidarity that the Holy Quran encourages from the believers. Assistance is done especially to relatives and sometimes without need being observed; alms or charity, rather, are forms of financial worship directed towards those without relatives in situations of destitution. These two are donations, cannot be returned, and God gives their reward. Benevolent loans are a loan given without expecting benefits other than the approval of God. In the provision of this debt, no benefit shall be expected from the indebted and only when the ability to repay arises shall the repayment of the debt be requested. Based on what we learned from the holy hadiths,[247] it

---

241 Enyclopedia of Miracles in Coran and Sunnah "Social Solidarity and Social Security in Islam" Translated by: Yasmin Muhammed Moslem, www.quran-m.com/firas/en1.

242 Suat Erdoğan, "Fıqh on Zakat Collection by Government", Journal of Islamic Legal Research, 2016, Issue: 28, (pp. 417–434), p. 418.

243 See Bakara, 2/275, 278, 279.

244 Turan, Yazgan, "Alms in Terms of Social Security", Journal of Turkic World Research, 1, Uludağ Printing, Istanbul June 1980, Issue: 6, Views, 135–136.

245 Beşer, Social Security in Islam, 1988, p. 256.

246 Bakara, 2/245.

247 The Prophet Muhammad proclaimed, "visiting the sick is to visit oneself, feeding the hungry is to feed oneself". (Müslim, Birr, 43)

encourages man for charitable works, beautiful acts, cooperation, and solidarity using an expression such that wherever and in whichever behaviors are found God's approval, He Himself is there."[248]

As a result, should the lives and cultures of individuals and societies become richer with the approaches and practices of the religion of Islam relating to social protection, they won't just remain stronger in their own constitution but will at the same time come into a situation that regulates the social peace of international societies. However, they will realize social solidarity and social protection with the newest institutions that they will gain for humanity.[249]

---

248 *The Way of the Quran*. Constructive Volume: 1, p. 385–386. https://kuran.diyanet.gov. tr/tefsir/Bakara-suresi/252/245-ayet-tefsiri

249 Şeker, p. 258.

2 The Basic Approaches (Principles) of Social Protection in Islamic Law

According to Islamic law, social protection encompasses very wide functions such as protecting the five universal values (zarûriyyât-ı hamse) in addition to the function of not just providing for economic assurance but at the same time for developing the personality of the individual.[250] For this reason, the fundamental approaches/principles for social protection in Islamic law are directly related to structural features[251] such as Islamic law being of divine origins, having the integrity of religion-morality-law, and foreseeing Earthly and heavenly sanctions. Principles such as divinity, worldliness and otherworldliness, morality, equality, environmental suitability, gaining the approval of the Creator, human love, tolerance, brotherhood of believers, social responsibility, and global validity/universalism, found in many verses in the Holy Quran[252] and in the hadiths of the Prophet Muhammad,[253] are essential in the social protection of individuals and society.

Primarily, these principles are directed towards correcting the mental structure and faith of people and were revealed in the Mecca period of the Prophet Muhammad, lasting 13 years. Such that, like the prior specification of the principles and fundamentals regarding each institution today, the principles of social protection were specified in Mecca.[254] Within the framework of these fundamentals, the belief structure of Muslims and the perspective of goods and humans is attempted to be corrected, and principal regulations were made in the dimension of public and human rights. All of these regulations were put into effect with the logic of Muslims resisting dangers and dividing/sharing the blessings together.[255] Later in the Medina period, in addition to awareness being

---

250 Okur, p. 314.
251 Köse, p. 26.
252 Bakara, 2/83–177–215–220, 266; Mâide, 5/2; İnsan, 76/8; Beled, 90/15–16; Ahzab, 33/72; Hucurât, 49/10; Tevbe, 9/60.
253 See Buhârî, "Nikâh", 91; "Cuma", 11; Cenâiz, 32; "Ahkâm", 1; Müslim, "İmâret", 20; Ebu Dâvûd, "İmâret", 1–13; Tirmizi, "Cihat", 27; Müslim, "İman", 74; Buhârî, "Nikâh", 45; "Edep", 57-58; "Ferâiz", 2; Müslim, "Birr", 28.
254 Sağlam, "A Summary Analysis on the Historical Roots of Today's Institution of Social Security", p. 132.
255 Sağlam, "A Summary Analysis on the Historical Roots of Today's Institution of Social Security", p. 35.

created by turning the principal foundations in question into consciousness, the activation of individual and societal conscience has been provided directed at implementation. Thus, as a result of legal regulations, moral rules should be transformed into the form of law.[256]

The principles and fundamental ideas in question that give meaning to the idea of the social state that Islamic law foresaw and that are the justifications for its remaining standing are mandatory for goodness, rights, and justice to be able to be sovereign in society. All of the socioeconomic relationships in society of the Islamic state must be organized so that all individuals take their shares of freedom, assurance, and honor. In this context, it is fundamental in Islamic law for people in society to develop their personalities in their work by encountering less obstacles and being encouraged and for all kinds of social protection for all citizens, Muslim and non-Muslims, to be provided. [257] In this framework, it is possible to see in many general principles and special provisions found in either the Holy Quran or in the words and example behaviors of the Prophet Muhammad that contain the fundamental approaches with regard to the outlook of Islamic law on humans, the world, and property, directed towards social protection.

I The Principle of Tawhid

The religion of Islam is a religion that is fundamentally a dynamic, realist, and innovative religion with a capacity for harmonizing with changing sociocultural conditions. The belief in tawhid/unity, which constitutes the fundamental creed of the religion of Islam, is a principle of the most wonderful and ideal social cohesion, interlocking, unification, integration, and, therefore, social protection.[258] There are numerous verses and hadiths from this commandment for unity. For example, it is proclaimed as such regarding unity in the Holy Quran: *"Say, O People of the Scripture, come to a word that is equitable between us and you - that we will not worship except Allah and not associate anything with Him and not take one another as lords instead of Allah..."*[259] In another verse, *"And who is better in religion than one who submits himself to Allah while being a doer of good and follows the religion of Abraham, inclining toward truth?..."*[260] With regard to

---

256 Saffet Köse, *Introduction to Islamic Law*, p. 53.

257 Esed, p. 26–27.; İbrahim Syed, Social Security in Islam, http://www.irfi.org/articles/articles_251_300/social_security_in_islam.htm (11. 05.2017).

258 Akyüz, p. 465.

259 Âl-i İmran, 3/64.

260 Nisâ, 4/125.

this matter, the Prophet Muhammad proclaimed that "*He who met Allah without associating anything with Allah entered Paradise and he who met Him associating (anything) with Him entered Fire.*"[261] Therefore, it is understood from verses and hadiths that tawhid/unity is commanded.

According to Islamic law, the concept of tawhid/unity as an indicative principle in social life means to be one, to be whole. This concept indicates the unity without separating into pieces in social life, there being a whole, undoubted compliance with the commandments of God, and there being a single body in fulfilling His commandments. This, as for example is in the commandment of alms,[262] is the protection of life and property from dangers with the principle of tawhid by fulfilling the individual and social responsibilities of Muslims with the spirit of tawhid in social life.[263]

In this framework, according to Islamic law, all humane living standards are under the assurance of the state, and labor is accepted as religious, and the equal identification of wage as the income of labor is valued. With regard to this matter, it is proclaimed in the Holy Quran that, "*And that there is not for man except that [good] for which he strives*".[264] However, individuals who are in society and partake in the distribution of income, who cannot work, and who are deprived of capital are to take their wages from the budget from the components of the indigent and sluggard. For this reason, together with a production predicated on property in the Islamic economy, there is an understanding of division that encompasses everybody in consumption and at the same time that gives individuals unable to produce the right to consume.[265] Sağlam evaluates this situation as the project of Muslims of the *division in blessings of participation in danger* and expresses it as the reflection of tawhid in social life. Thus, the belief of tawhid as a principle that ensures the realization of social justice expresses security and assurance for humanity and contributes to social justice and social protection.[266]

---

261 Müslim, "İman", 93.

262 Tevbe, 113/60.

263 Sağlam, "A Summary Analysis on the Historical Roots of Today's Institution of Social Security", p. 133.

264 Necm, 53/39.

265 Yusuf Temür, The Institution of Negative Taxes in the Scope of the Welfare State and of Alms in the Economy of Islam, *BJSS Balkan Journal of Social Sciences*, 6, Issue: 12, p. 2.

266 Sağlam, "A Summary Analysis on the Historical Roots of Today's Institution of Social Security", p. 133.

II The Principle of Morality

The ultimate goal of the societal order of Islam is to prevent oppression and injustice for people and to foresee sustaining justice on Earth, with the verse of, *"You are the best nation produced [as an example] for mankind. You enjoin what is right and forbid what is wrong and believe in Allah...",*[267] which constitutes the foundation of the moral principles of Islamic society. In this context, the hadiths of the Prophet Muhammad of *"If man enjoys how others are treated, how he himself is treated, let him act as such"*[268] and *"There shall be no such thing as harming others or responding to harm with harm"*[269] are the universal principles of morality that will be valid always and everywhere directed towards social protection in society.

We should especially indicate here that, while social security is entirely evaluated today as a material and economic phenomenon, it is assessed as a phenomenon directed towards worship and morals in addition to being economic.[270] Because merely legal rules are insufficient in the organization of societal life and in the provision of social protection in society. The law deals with and regulates the outer-facing aspect of the individual and societal behaviors of people. In this situation, the legal norm shall be implemented to the objective side, to incidences in which the behavior occurs in the outer world. However, morals deal with the inward-facing aspect of the behaviors in question of man, man being effective in his inner world is the conscientious situation of the person. [271] On this matter, the Holy Quran draws attention to the feelings of conscience with the expression, *"it is not eyes that are blinded, but blinded are the hearts which are within the breasts."*[272]

Legal rules generally see the duty of the register of security behind moral rules. For example, as a rule of law, whoever suffers loss should get one's due from whoever caused the loss. However, regarding a rule of morality, its forgiveness is more charitable. Again, according to Islamic law, the owner and proprietor of that which people earn. However, it is a moral rule that other people may be allowed to benefit from this property.[273] In addition to this, when a person's

---

267 Âl-i İmrân, 3/110.
268 Müslim, "İmâre", 46.
269 İbn Mâce, "Ahkâm", 17.
270 Beşer, Social Security in Islam, 2016, p. 206.
271 Ayten Erol, "Gaining Moral Values from an Islamic Jurisprudence Perspective", *Kırıkkale University Journal of Social Sciences (KUSBD)*, 6, July 2016, Issue: 2, (pp. 229–254), p. 234.
272 Hajj, 22/46.
273 Tabakoğlu, p. 13.

time comes, they have the right to ask for what they shall receive. In addition to this need for law and justice, its extension of the duration or its donation in situations of need is the recommendation of religion.[274] Transforming this into a way of life is a moral behavior that is commendable from the perspective of Islam."[275] In other words, when a rule of morality relies on legal sanction and punishment, it anymore becomes a rule of law. To steal, to not pay one's debt is an example of this. However, in contrary to this, a legal sanction that will compel whoever doesn't comply with the rule of morality is not the point in question. For example, nobody can legally be punished because they didn't give bread to someone face-to-face with death by hunger. Because to give bread to an impoverished person is not a legal but moral duty.[276] In this situation, the conscience relies on the two fundamentals that constitute religion and morality that form the moral aspect of man, and thus religion and morality ensure immaterial sanction on law, and strength is gained to the scale that it relies on the principles of law, religion, and morality.[277] Thus, immaterial strength both brings feelings of connection to the teachings given with stable self-control and the ability for implementation and provides important contributions to the provision of societal order.[278] And the importance of the formation of a legal system based on the divine, of Islamic law, shows itself here.

In this context, to think of another, according to Islamic law, is moral fact; for example, as much a Muslim in the west thinking of the thorn that has pierced the foot of a Muslim in the east as economic and material. Likewise, the prohibition of illegitimate means of production, alms, charities, and taxes, the aid that must be given to relatives, penances, and the incentives and obligations[279] by way of aiding beyond what is needed with help for the needy carry moral qualities as much as economic.[280]

---

274 Bakara, 2/280.
275 Köse, *Introduction to Islamic Law*, p. 49.
276 Hayreddin, Karaman, *Comparative Islamic Law*, vol. I–III, Bayrak Printing, Istanbul 1991, I/10, 11.
277 Saffet Köse, "Is it Law or Morality? Research in the Context of the Religion-Morals-Law Relationship from Islam Viewpoint", *Journal of Islamic Legal Research*, Konya 2011, Issue: 17, p. 9.
278 Abdurrahman Candan, "Oath and Morality in Islamic Law", *Journal of Islamic Legal Research*, 2010, Issue: 15, (pp. 431–452), p. 438.
279 Bakara, 2/177; Tevbe, 9/103.
280 Yılmaz, p. 157.

According to the religion of Islam, one of the important moral traits that contributes to social protection and that must be found in the virtuous believer is conviction. Conviction as a moral term that means to approve of, to content oneself with what's in one's hand means to make do with the material opportunities with which people may maximally meet the needs of those under themselves and their responsibility and to be rescued from the envy of what is in the hands of others and from the greed of excessive gain.[281] Because greed,[282] as a phenomenon that exists in the disposition of man, is the opposite of conviction and expresses a hunger and discontent that will not be satisfied, a want and a desire that knows no end. Especially greed whose balance cannot be established may be the correspondent of great individual and societal disasters, including ambitious people, and the conclusion of extreme greed is deprivation.[283] For this reason, the Prophet Muhammad drew attention to this danger by stating that a person won't be satisfied even if they have two valleys full of gold and that nothing will fill the bellies/desires of humanity other than earth by saying that they will want a third.[284]

The words of "The cause of hunger and misery on Earth is not the inability to satisfy the impoverished but the inability to satisfy the rich!" is quite meaningful in this context. Therefore, according to Islamic law, a condition of both protecting human personality and dignity and developing and living happily and peacefully[285] is to hold a belief in the never-ending treasure. In this context, justice, security, and welfare in the distribution of income must be propagated, individuals must be able to capture a balance between their resources and needs, and ensuring they have belief is necessary.[286] Because one who believes should hold conviction, should be thankful for the sustenance that God has esteemed to him after working and after referring to reasons. Because true wealth is the satiation of the eye and desire of people.

281 Mustafa Çağrıcı, "Belief", *Islamic Encyclopedia of Diyanet*, 2001, XXIV/289-290.

282 Meâric, 70/19.

283 Sabri Erturhan, "The Moral Principles that Give Body to Islamic Commercial Law", *Journal of Islamic Legal Research*, XVI, Islamic Economics Special Issue, Issue: 16, Konya 2010, XVI/213–246, p. 237.

284 See Buhârî, Rikâk, 10; Müslim, Zekât, 116–119; Tirmizî, Zühd, 27, "Menâkıb, 64; İbn Mâce, "Zühd, 27.

285 Çağrıcı, "Belief", *IED*, XXIV/290.

286 Yazıcı, p. 7.

As is to be understood from all these examples, we can say that the moral behaviors and relationships looking to be created among the individuals of society are directed towards contributing to the social protection of society.

III The Principle of Property

In this framework, it is possible to see the fundamental approaches with regard to the outlook of Islamic law on property, directed towards social protection, in many general principles and special provisions found in either the Holy Quran or in the words and example behaviors of the Prophet Muhammad.

According to Islamic law, the actual owner of assets/property is God. While the property that God granted to his servants is the trust given to them, the assets and people are the "trustees".[287] In many verses in the Holy Quran[288] such as the verse of *"establish prayer, and spend out of what We have provided for them,"*[289] it is expressed that God is the true owner of property and that the blessings of people given to themselves in their worldly lives are spent in His way and how He wishes. Again, with regard to this matter in the Holy Quran, it was proclaimed that, *"But seek, through that which Allah has given you, the home of the Hereafter; and [yet], do not forget your share of the world. And do good as Allah has done good to you..."*[290]. Again, with regard to the matter of using assets and property given to oneself on behalf of God in line with His approval, it was proclaimed *"... And whatever you spend of good - it will be fully repaid to you, and you will not be wronged."*[291]

In this context, there primarily is labor in the foundations of property, according to Islamic law.[292] The labor of people, goods they produce, and their great efforts are worship of service.[293] The Prophet Muhammad proclaimed: *"Give the worker his wages before his sweat dries."*[294] Therefore, the products of other factors of production such as capital and earth may reside with the individual along with the labor and support of people. Man doesn't have the right to do whatever he

---

287 Ahzâb, 33/72.
288 Al-i İmran, 3/26; En'am, 6/151; İbrahim, 14/2; Furkan, 25/2; Kehf, 18/46; Yunus, 10/55.
289 Bakara, 2/3.
290 Kasas, 28/77.
291 Bakara, 2/272.
292 Necm 53/ 39; Nisâ, 4/32.
293 Osman Eskicioğlu, "Economic System in Islam", *Journal of Islamic Legal Research*, Issue: 16, 2010, (pp. 35–46), p. 44.
294 İbn Mâce, II/817.

likes in his property.[295] Man has the right to private property.[296] However, private property must not interfere with societal interests. For this reason, public property was envisaged over energy resources, strategic minerals, wide agricultural earth. Here, in the scope of the zarûrât-ı hamse in Islamic law, pursuant to the principle of the "protection of property", both the protection of property from attacks and the avoidance of its waste and destruction are points in question. In addition to this, one of the most important objectives of Islamic economics is to prevent the propagation of private property and the collection in certain hands. For this reason, inheritance should be made to be shared among as many relatives as possible.[297] When the affairs of society in Islamic law are the point in question, private property can be struggled with. In situations of necessity, new limitations can be placed temporarily on personal property. For example, after the hijrah to Medina, a brotherhood was established between the migrants and the ansars, the ansars gave a portion of their wealth to the migrants, and their profits were made common. After the conquering of the Khyber Pass, these goods were given back to their old owners.[298] Pursuant to necessity here, the struggle with private property directed to the social protection of society became the point in question.[299]

On the other hand, the economic system is, according to Islamic law, a system in which property is applied in production, joint ownership in consumption, and principles of alms in partnership and taxes.[300] In this framework, the impoverished and destitute have rights in the property of whoever has wealth.[301] In other words, the social protection of the destitute segments of society is ensured by means of the wealthy segments of society. At this point, the approach of the religion of Islam in terms of its perspective on people carries great importance. It is proclaimed in the Holy Quran that, *"...It is We who have apportioned among them their livelihood in the life of this world and have raised some of them above others in degrees [of rank] that they may make use of one another for service..."*[302] The fact that skills, income, and strength between people are different is

---

295 Hûd, 11/87–88.

296 *"...There is a share to men from what they have earned..." There is a share for women from what they have earned..."* (Nisâ, 4/32).

297 Nisâ, 4/176.

298 Buhârî, "İcâre", 2.

299 Tabakoğlu, p. 27.

300 Eskicioğlu, p. 44, 45.

301 Zariyât 51/19; Meâric 70/24–25; En'am, 6/141.

302 Zuhrûf, 43/32.

not a reason for superiority but is a vehicle for the trial of human life.[303] Therefore, Islamic belief considers human life as a moral trial,[304] and as voluntary sharing with other people when necessary by lawfully gaining assets and property.[305]

The Prophet Muhammad proclaimed in one of his hadiths that, "*God does not look at your outward appearance and your assets; He only looks at your heart and your works*".[306] There is no superiority based on race, gender, property, or assets. People are created to be devoted to material goods, [307] are in different conditions, and are responsible based on these conditions.[308]

According to Karaman, who states that the measurement in which the Quran is used while evaluating human understanding and people prevents the formation of classes in Muslim society, creating a social class within the religion of Islam and society indicates that there are great philosophies in the existence of the impoverished, the rich, and of different people in terms of science, merit, and skill. In addition to this, Karaman states that what the Holy Quran is asking is not to provide economic equality among all people by removing poverty but to guarantee the natural needs of the impoverished and to prevent with permanent measures the negative effects and results on people of poverty, and he lists some of these measures as such: "a) To ensure that those with opportunities to work find work, work, and produce and thus eliminate their needs. b) To help individuals work in the field where they are competent and capable and be efficient by considering the various needs for work and activities of society, from unskilled labor to engineering, education, management, and military. c) To ensure that those who are unable to resolve their needs by working and developing their capabilities live at a level of life and welfare that suits people." The most important sources of this are beytülmâl (the treasury, assets of the state), alms, and the contribution of alimony among relatives."[309]

---

303 En'am, 6/165.
304 "And We will surely test you with something of fear and hunger and a loss of wealth and lives and fruits, but give good tidings to the patient," (Bakara, 2/155); Âl-i İmrân, 3/186; Enfâl, 8/28; Kehf, 18/7; Casiye, 45/22; Teğabün, 64/15.
305 Nesimi Yazıcı, "The Social Market Economic and its Perception in Islam", 7, Çalıştay, Ankara 2010. http://www.kas.de/wf/doc/kas_23417-1522-12-30.pdf?110816144640. (14.03.2018)
306 Müslim, "Birr", 34.
307 Fecr, 89/20.
308 Ahzâb, 33/72.
309 Hayreddin Karaman, "Social Justice". https://www.yenisafak.com/yazarlar/hayrettinkaraman/sosyal-adalet-2038715. (12.03. 2018)

In this context, Tabakoğlu states that an aristocracy of the earth and a bourgeoisie of industry and commerce didn't form in Islamic society, and said, "They created a small-scale but common industrial system in the artisan institutions that are connected to the tradition of the futuwwa (chivalry) and ahis (Turkish-Islamic Guild). The quality of Islam that prevents class division is stable with the role that it plays in the development of social service institutions like foundations.[310] Thus, the income excess of people was transferred to institutions of social service by themselves. Therefore, the aim is to not waste the strength of being able to pay more than its value to a good, known technically as consumer income, in luxurious consumption (in the form of excess fares in vehicles of transportation, touristic rates, expenses well above the public standard) and to help improve societal welfare."[311]

IV The Principle of Justice

As one of the most important objectives of social protection in Islamic law, justice means to click something into place, to give the rights to each right holder, and it is both a legal and a moral term.[312] The epithet of God is the commandment of the Holy Quran,[313] and justice, as one of the justifications for sending the prophets,[314] is an element of peace and trust in individual and societal life. It is the foundation of property, sovereignty, and societal life.[315] In this context, justice is expressed as avoiding extravagance and understatement (excessiveness) in either belief and word or in actions and choosing the middle road.[316]

---

310 For example, dervish lodge structures and foundations administer an important function in the point of the protection of the zarûrât-ı hamse. Foundation services at Anatolian dervish lodges represent an economic strength that is as effective as it is religious with its agricultural-industrial operations and social assistance functions. In relation to this, the Anatolian dervish lodge kitchens are an indicator of a dynamic unique to themselves that combine material structure and immaterial dimension in terms of social protection. (Güldane Gündüzöz, *The Motif of Food in Bektashi Culture*, Ataturk Cultural Center Publications, Ankara 2015, p. 118)

311 Tabakoğlu, p. 26.

312 Erturhan, p. 219; Nasi Aslan, "On the Civilization of Justice", *Journal of Islamic Legal Research*, 2016, Issue: 28, (pp. 9–27), p. 10.

313 Nahl, 16/90; A'râf, 7/29.

314 Hadîd, 57/25.

315 Erturhan, p. 219.

316 Aslan, p. 10.

Indeed, justice attained and intended to be realized with all varieties in the Holy Quran means the power and opportunities which God makes reference to for man being balanced by society, the reference to the rights of every person within this balance, and the realization of humanity.[317] With regard to this matter, along with the verse, *"Indeed, Allah orders justice and good conduct and giving to relatives and forbids immorality and bad conduct and oppression..."*[318] it is proclaimed in the Holy Quran: *"And weigh with an even balance. And do not deprive people of their due and do not commit abuse on earth, spreading corruption."*[319] Therefore, "justice", as it is understood from these verses, is a moral virtue meaning suitability and accuracy to the principles of rights, law, fairness, and equality. In addition to this, it is a legal term that states that all people are created equally and that therefore everyone deserves to live in social welfare in line with equality of opportunity.[320] However, it will not suit fairness, as that which is equal for everybody being provided and everyone being subjected to equal process gives rise to the result of the breakdown of equality in some situations, because individuals are not in equal situations with one another in terms of their needs, capabilities, and opportunities. For example, not the mother who gives each child the same amount and type of food but the mother who gives the older child more and different types of food will be deemed just. Likewise, not equal types of taxes but taxes taken based on earnings are befitting taxes. On the other hand, the provision of what is equal to those in the same situation will befit the idea of equality.[321]

Justice in Islamic law expresses the balance that which is generally given and that which is deserved, and it is stated that this balance is carried out equally in some situations but that justice, not equality, is balance.[322] According to Karaman, "The measure is not equality but balance in the understanding of social justice, which relies on principles like property belonging to God, man and especially believers bring brothers, the impoverished and destitute having rights in individual wealth, and God commanding beneficence and which allows everybody

---

317 Karaman, "Social Justice", https://www.yenisafak.com/yazarlar/hayrettinkaraman/ sosyal-adalet-2038715 (10.01.2018)

318 16. Nahl, 90.

319 26. Şu'arâ, 182–183.

320 Ali Fuat Akçapınar, http://www.mirathaber.com/ali-fuat-akcapinar-islam-siyasetinde-bir-sosyal-devlet-modeli-var-midir-22-467y.html (30.01.2018)

321 Aslan, p. 13.

322 Hayreddin Karaman, "justice", (Islamic Law), *Islamic Encyclopedia of Diyanet*, 1988, (I/343–344) p. 343; Aslan, p. 17.

to live as people and to procure their needs without considering the economic and social situation of people within society."[323]

The hadith of the Prophet Muhammad encouraging justice in the shaped of: "*Those who act justly towards those under subjugation, their families, and those under servitude are above the pulpits from the light on the day of judgement*"[324] is in a broad sense and covers moral, legal, and social justice.[325] Therefore, directed at social protection in Islamic law, the establishment of social justice and social balance by providing for equality among powerful societal groups and weak and dependent groups in economic terms.[326] In other words, that the rich not become richer and the poor not become poorer is a fundamental condition for the provision of social justice and social protection. For the realization of social justice and social protection, compromising on waste, the just division of income, the propagation of wealth and property, and economic stability are fundamental. These fundamentals are, at the same time, moral principles. Because waste means both disrespect to labor, an important factor in production, and to humans and disrespect to nature and the environment.[327]

Indeed, the Prophet Muhammad indicated that man must establish a balance of Earth and the afterlife while making the recommendation of "*Work for your world as if you will never die, work for the afterlife as if you will die tomorrow.*"[328] Therefore, justice expresses the balance between the world and the afterlife as a lifestyle.

In this framework individuals thinking of the needs of others together with their own needs, working to establish balance between these two, refraining from stinginess and from waste, and preferring compromise in meeting their needs just as in other areas of their life are all envisaged, directed towards social protection in Islamic law.[329] Also, in addition to the preservation of individual rights in Islamic law, it holds individuals responsible for society. In this context, pursuant to one of the hadiths of the Prophet Muhammad, an individual should prevent evil when he sees it, whether big or small, first with his hand and then with his tongue if his strength does not suffice. If his strength doesn't

---

323 Karaman, "justice", (Islamic Law), *IED*, I/343.

324 Müslim, İmâre, 18.

325 Aslan, p. 13.

326 Kapar, p. 5. www.sosyalkoruma.net(12.10.2017)

327 Tabakoğlu, p. 22.

328 Ahmed Ziyaeddin Gümüşhanevî, *Râmuzu'l-Ehâdis*, Hemze md. 75/1.

329 Rahmi Yaran, *The Concept and Institutionalization of Need in Islamic Law*, Marmara University Faculty of Divinity Foundation Publications, Istanbul 2007, p. 41

suffice for this, he should denigrate it with his heart.[330] According to the religion of Islam, when oppression appears in society, the person who is not oppressing but does nothing to prevent it is as responsible as those who are oppressing.[331] Therefore, in the scope of the preservation of the zarurât-ı hamse directed at the provision of social protection in Islamic law, it is a necessity of justice for sensibility relating to the principle of retaining reactions shown against injustice and oppression and goodness from order and evil.[332]

V The Principle of Brotherhood

As it is known, the people dispersing from Adam and Eve constitute in time, great and small societies/nations in various colors and languages on Earth. Regarding this matter, it is proclaimed in the Holy Quran as such: *"O mankind, indeed We have created you from male and female and made you peoples and tribes that you may know one another. Indeed, the most noble of you in the sight of Allah is the most righteous of you. Indeed, Allah is Knowing and Acquainted."*[333] As it is to be understood from the verse, societies that differ greatly until they arrive at nations from clans are wanted to know one another, to understand and socialize one another, rather than to boast about with their own kindred or races. Man, according to the religion of Islam, is responsible to God in accordance with his purpose for creation[334] in immaterial and social terms against people and the social environment.[335] These individuals assuming their responsibilities are not like ordinary members of a society but the organs of a body, of whom the pain of one affects all. While immaterial/otherworldly brotherhood[336] is the point in question should the individuals that constitute society pursuant to the responsibility they have assumed be of the same religion, should they not be of the same religion, brotherhood is the point in question in the Earthly/legal sense.[337] Indeed, the Prophet Muhammad proclaimed that *"You shall see believers just as a in a body in loving one another, in being compassionate to one another, in*

---

330 See Ebû Dâvûd, Salat, 1140; Melâhim, 4340.
331 Tabakoğlu, p. 21.
332 Aslan, p. 16.
333 Hucurât, 49/13.
334 Zârîyat, 51/56.
335 Kıyame, 75/36.
336 Hucurât 49/10.
337 Ali Fuat Akçapınar, http://www.mirathaber.com/ali-fuat-akcapinar-islam-siyasetinde-bir-sosyal-devlet-modeli-var-midir-22-467y.html (30.01.2018)

being charitable to one another; (meaning) that if one part falls ill, the other parts join together in his illness with restlessness and fervor.[338]. In another one of the hadiths, the Prophet Muhammad said *"All people, all of you are the sons of God; Adam was created from the earth. People shall cease to boast with their fathers and grandfathers. Because those who act as such are more worthless than a small ant in the eyes of God."*[339]

Indeed, "The Hijrah incident, which took place in the first years of Islam, constitutes one of the first and most important examples of the phenomenon of social solidarity in Islamic society. During the Hijrah, an incredibly important hadith in Islamic history, the Muslims migrating from Mecca to Medina were exposed to great struggles, and at the end of a troublesome journey, they reached Median despite having left all their property in Mecca. The people encountering them in Medina almost competed with one another on the issue of helping and offering and put forth everything they possessed to meet the needs of these people coming from Mecca. This example of the solidarity that the Muslims in Medina displayed was glorified in the Holy Quran[340] and shown as an example to other Muslims."[341]

As is to be seen, the perspective on humans of the Holy Quran and of the Prophet Muhammad resides upon the fraternity of people, derived from the existence of his respectable reverence[342] and from a mother-father. In this context, according to Islamic law, all people are the children of mothers and fathers and are brothers in terms of being human.[343] Therefore, pursuant to the principle of brotherhood, should nations try to understand one another in the framework of mutual respect and reconcile in a civilized manner on issues where they do not see eye to eye, the formation of global peace and earthly and legal brotherhood is possible in the international dimension. In addition to this, it was proclaimed in the Holy Quran directed to Muslims: *"And hold firmly to the rope of Allah all together and do not become divided. And remember the favor of Allah upon you- when you were enemies and He brought your hearts together and you became, by His favor, brothers. And you were on the edge of a pit of the Fire, and He saved you from it. Thus does Allah make clear to you His verses that you may*

---

338 Buhârî, Edeb, 27.
339 Ebû Dâvûd, Edeb, 111.
340 Haşr, 59/9.
341 Akyüz, p. 465; Beşer, Social risk-danger, p. 50.
342 İsrâ, 17/70.
343 Saffet Köse, "The Summit of Prestige Because of the Humanity of Humans in Muslim Thought", *Journal of Islamic Legal Research*, Konya 2009, Issue: 14, (pp. 49–66), p. 50.

be guided.".[344] Therefore, as is to be understood from this verse, the relationships between Muslims must rely on the principles of intimacy/recognition/introduction/dialog that in turn rely on peace and legal brotherhood. Thus, for world peace, being able to provide for this mutual intimacy and double/multiple compromise is dependent on Muslims forming among themselves the law of *spiritual brotherhood.*[345] In this context, it is clear that all of humanity is in a fraternal relationship according to Islamic law and that the principle of brotherhood will contribute to the social protection of all of humanity should it be implemented.

There is no doubt that these fundamental principles and approaches that we expressed towards the provision of the social protection of individuals and society will be carry importance to the degree that people are dependent on their religiosity and religious provisions and will allow for the desired results to be attained at the point of implementation.[346]

---

344 Âl-i İmrân, 3/103.
345 Ali Fuat Akçapınar, http://www.mirathaber.com/ali-fuat-akcapinar-islam-siyasetinde-bir-sosyal-devlet-modeli-var-midir-22-467y.html (30.01.2018)
346 Armağan, p. 83.

Conclusion

The worldview of the religion of Islam towards social life and social problems is the social policy of Islamic law. The entirety of the theoretic and practical provisions that the religion of Islam recommends for social policy, social justice, and social protection constitute the social aspect of Islamic law.

Along with there not being a standard model for a social law state in Islam, a state that will ensure societal order composed of the entirety of religion, law, and morality, foreseen by Islamic law, that establishes its base on and serves the welfare of society and a legal state predicated on equality are the two fundamental principles of the Islamic social state model. The social state is responsible for the provision of social protection.

Even if its name as a concept is not "social security" or "social protection" as it is today, social protection begins with the creation of man as a universal phenomenon, according to Islamic law.

Social justice aims to bring individuals and society to a level of healthy, peaceful, and just welfare both materially and immaterially, by taking precautions that allow people to live as the people that God created as reverence (mükerrem).

The purpose for the sending of the religion of Islam is affairs. Meaning, to protect these by realizing the things that lead to the benefit of society and removing the matters that lead to the damage of people, in accordance with this. The affairs regarding societal needs according to Islamic law are composed of the imperative needs (zarûriyyât), normal needs (haciyyât), beautifier needs (tahsiniyyât) of people.

According to Islamic law, the provision of the tranquility and social protection of humanity is dependent on the provision of affairs (life, property, lineage, intellect, and religion) referred to by names such as "zarûriyyat-ı hamse", "makasıd-ı hamse", and "külliyyat-ı hams". The ability to provide social protection all over the world and the absolute protection of these five universal values is imperative for all humanity, whether believers or not.

Risks and dangers towards the life, property, intellect, lineage, and religion of people, beyond the willpower of people and for which it is uncertain when they will materialize, constitute the issue of social protection in Islamic law.

According to Islamic law, social protection means both the prevention of risks and dangers before they emerge and the development of the personality regarding the preservation of the five universal values of *zarûriyyat-ı hamse* and the individual and institutional meeting of all the needs of people for the preservation of these five universal values.

While the aim is the "Protection of people, for people" in the understandings today of social protection, the purpose of social protection according to Islamic law is, primarily, the "protection of people for (the approval of) God." Because not just a worldly profit but at the same time benefit for the afterlife in all work that man does in accordance with religion, because religious sanctions observe not just the world but also the afterlife. Social protection is important in terms of being able to sustainable provide that which exists by protecting these values from all types of danger and risk and thus realizing social justice and social peace in society.

Both individuals and the state are responsible for the preservation of the *zarûriyyat-ı hamse*, the five universal values, directed at social protection, according to Islamic law. The expense of effort by a person who believes is not just for his or her own security but for the security of society and all of humanity and is the necessity for faith/belief; especially *the belief in the afterlife* is the greatest assurance for social protection.

The choice of the middle road is envisaged in the acts of individuals thinking of the needs of others together with their own needs, working to establish balance between these two, refraining from stinginess and waste, and meeting their needs just like they do in other areas of their lives, directed towards social protection in Islamic law.

According to the religion of Islam, the greatest honor given to people is to be the caliph of God. Being the caliph to God is to have the authority to judge things on His behalf. Because humans are the most honorable of creation, in because man is the most honorable of creation and was created in the most beautiful form in existence (ahsen-i takvim). Man is worthy because he is man. Superiority is but doing good works with piety.

According to the religion of Islam, the actual owner of assets/property is God. The property that God has granted to his servants is the trust given to them. Assets and people, however, are the "trustees". In this situation, a rich Muslim does not have unlimited freedom on matters of spending his own property, according to Islamic law. The destitute and poor have rights in the personal wealth of the rich.

According to Islamic law, no matter how dangerous poverty and destitution that results in forgetting to fulfill the duties of servitude for God are in terms of social peace and social justice, wealth that exacerbates and dampens social responsibility and sensitivity is just as extreme of a social danger.

In the scope of the zarûriyyat-ı hamse in Islamic law, pursuant to the principle of the "protection of property", both the protection of property from attacks and the avoidance of its waste and destruction are necessary.

According to Islam, the fact that there are differences in skill, income, and strength between people is not a reason for superiority. These are vehicles for the examination of human life. Belief in Islam is assessed in the form of a trial in terms of morality of human life and of voluntarily sharing with other people when necessary by legitimately earning assets and property.

In Islamic law, even if it materializes with equality in some situations, is not equality but balance. All humans are created equal. Everybody has the right to live in social welfare, in line with equality of opportunity. However, because what is equal being provided and everyone being subjected to equal work produces the result of the degradation of equality in some situations due to there being differences among individuals in terms of the needs, talents, and opportunities of individuals, it is not suitable for fairness.

According to the religion of Islam, a condition of people both protecting and developing their personality and dignity and living a happy and peaceful life is having conviction, belief. Justice, security, and welfare must be propagated in the distribution of income, people must be able to capture a balance among their resources and needs, and they must have conviction. One who believes should hold conviction, should be thankful for the sustenance that God has esteemed to him after working and after referring to reasons. Because true wealth is the satiation of the eye and desires of people.

When considering that the social security/protection systems of today work to provide social protection directed towards the general security of life and property and that they cannot provide adequate protection in the face of risks and of whatever lays beyond these; in Islamic law, not just the maintenance of physical experience by people for the provision of societal justice, equality, and peace but in the scope of the social protection for anybody in need for the protection of the zarûriyyat-ı hamse (life, property, lineage, intellect, religion) which are necessary for society to remain upright.

The understandings of *social cooperation* and *social solidarity* constitute the fundamental principles of social protection in Islamic law. With social solidarity, the feeling is gained that each individual in society has a set of duties and responsibilities that they must fulfill for themselves and for society. The understanding settles that there is a set of rights of individuals and society against one another with this feeling. The awareness of duty formed within the framework of the value of belief and the sensibility of accountability in individuals constitutes the most effective way for these rights to be guaranteed.

Islamic law aims for the social development of society by making dominant feelings of tawhid/unity, justice, brotherhood, social solidarity, sharing, and cooperation, for the creation of a social order that ensures people fulfill their duties of servitude for God, and for sustainable development.

Islamic law partakes in a system of both formation in stages of division of income pursuant to the principle of there not being power that wanders into the hands of a certain class of the rich, at the point where the principles and approaches directed at social protection are implemented. In this context, in order to reduce the difference between wealth in society and social strata, they create a system of social protection in which numerous regulations and institutions of social protection, along with social justice, are provided, being both *compulsory* and *voluntary*, such as the prohibition of trafficking and interest and the encouragement of alms and assistance.

The implementation of regulations directed towards social protection in Islamic law in Muslim societies today is seen as a reason to increase the need for social protection.

According to Islamic law, all people are the children of a mother and father and are brothers and sisters in terms of being human. While *immaterial/other-worldly* brotherhood is the point in question should the individuals who constitute society be of the same religion, pursuant to the responsibilities they have assumed, *worldly/legal* brotherhood is the point in question should they be of different religions.

Nations should make an effort to understand one another in the framework of mutual respect and should be able to mediate in a civilized manner on issues upon which they cannot agree, pursuant to the principle of brotherhood for the provision of social protection around the world. However, it could be possible for global peace and worldly/legal brotherhood to be created in this manner in an international dimension. According to Islamic law, the implementation of the principle of brotherhood will contribute to the social protection of all humanity.

In order for social protection to be able to be provided all over the world, according to Islamic law, the approaches and fundamental principles regarding the *outlook* on *man, property, and life* of the religion of Islam must be known and implemented. The implementation of these fundamental principles and approaches carry importance to the degree of the religiosity of people and their dependence on religious provisions and will reach the desired results.

Should the life and culture of individuals and societies enrichen with the fundamental approaches, principles, and applications of Islamic law regarding social protection, not only will it be strong within its own constitution but will at the same time become a regulator of the social peace of international societies. However, they will realize social solidarity and social protection with the newest institutions that they will gain for humanity.

Bibliography

Aclûnî, İsmâil b. Muhammed, (A.D. 1162/1749), *Keşfu'l-Hafâ*, Beirut 1351.

Ahmed b. Hanbel, *el-Müsned*, Çağrı Publication, Istanbul 1982, I-VI.

Akçapınar, Ali Fuat, http://www.mirathaber.com/ali-fuat-akcapinar-islam-siyasetinde-bir-sosyal-devlet-modeli-var-midir-22-467y.html (30.01.2018)

Akyıldız, Hüseyin, *Social Security Law*, Süleyman Demirel University Publication No: 43, Faculty of Economics and Sciences, Isparta 2004.

Akyüz, Vecdi, Mehmet Erdoğan, İz Publishing House, Istanbul 1996.

Akyüz, İsmail, "The Effect of Societal Solidarity of Religious Practices in Islam", *The Journal of Academic Social Science: Studies International Journal of Social Science*, Number 25-I, p. 461-482, Summer I 2014.

Armağan, Servet, "Basic Institutions of Social Security in the Religion of Islam", *Journal of Islamic Legal Research*, Issue: 14, Dumat Ofset Publishing San. Com. Ltd. Co., Ankara 2009.

Aslan, Nasi, "On the Civilization of Justice", *Journal of Islamic Legal Research*, 2016, Issue: 28, pp. 9-27.

Aykanat, Mehmet, Fundamental Institutions in Ottoman Social Security Law, Selçuk University Institute of Social Sciences, *Unprinted Doctoral Thesis*, Konya 2015.

Aynî, Ebû Muhammed Bedruddîn Mahmud b. Ahmed, (A.D. 855) *Umdetu'l-Kârî*, Matbaa-i Âmire, (publication place not available), 1308, I-XI.

Belen, Fatıma Zeynep Belen, "Immaterial and Psychosocial Practices of Care for Disadvantaged Groups: The Example of Sevilla", *Immaterial and Psychosocial Care for Disadvantaged Groups*, Editors: İhsan Çapçıoğlu, Fatıma Zeynep Belen, Grafiker Publications, Ankara 2016.

Beşer, Faruk, *Social Security in Islam*, Nûn, Publishing House, Istanbul 2016.

Beşer, Faruk, *Social Security in Islam*, Seha Neşriyat, Temel Press, Istanbul 1988.

Beşer, Faruk, Social Risks Insurance and Islam http://sosyalsiyaset.net/documents/sosyal_riskler_sigorta_ve_islam.htm (12.06.2018)

Beşer, Faruk, *Women's Studies and Social Security in Islam*, Nûn Publishing House, Kilim Press, Istanbul 2009.

Beşer, Faruk, *Social Security in Islam*, Nûn Publishing House, Istanbul 2016.

Buhâri, Ebû Abdillâh Muhammed b. İsmâîl, *Sahihu'l- Buhâri*, el-Mektebetü'l-İslâmiyye, Istanbul (publication date not available), I–VIII.

Boynukalın, Ertuğrul, "Makâsıdu'ş-Şerîa", *Islamic Encyclopedia of Diyanet*, 2003, XXVII, 423-427.

Bozkurt, Nebi, "Himâye", *Islamic Encyclopedia of Diyanet*, 1998, XVIII/56.

Bûtî, Muhammed Saîd Ramazan, *Davâbıtu'l-Maslaha fi'ş-Şerîati'l-İslâmiyye*, Müessesetü'r-Risâle, Beirut 1402/1982.

Candan, Abdurrahman, "Oath and Morality in Islamic Law", *Journal of Islamic Legal Research*, 2010, Issue: 15, pp. 431–452.

Cessâs, Ebû Bekir Ahmed, (A.D. 370–980), *Ahkâmu'l-Kur'ân*, thk. Muhammed es-Sâdık Kamhâvî, Beirut 1405/1985.

Cüveynî, Abdülmelik b. Abdullah b. Yusuf, (A.D. 1085), *el-Burhân*, Dâru'l-Kütübi'l-İlmiyye, Beirut–Lebanon 1997.

Çağrıcı, Mustafa, "zaruriyyât", *Islamic Encyclopedia of Diyanet*, 2013, XLIV/146–148.

Çağrıcı, Mustafa, "Belief", *Islamic Encyclopedia of Diyanet*, 2001, XXIV/289–290.

Çalış, Halit, "Zaruret", *Islamic Encyclopedia of Diyanet*, 2013, XLIV/141–144.

Çalış, Halit, "Islam and Human Rights: The Duty-Prioritized Model of Society", *Notices of the Human Rights and Religion Symposium*, 15–17May 2009, Çanakkale Onsekiz Mart University Publications, Çanakkale 2010.

Çalış, Halit, "Zaruret", *Islamic Encyclopedia of Diyanet*, XLIV, 2013, pp. 141–144.

Çambel, Ayça, Social Poverty and Social Protection in the Era of Globalization, Ege University, Department of Economics, Faculty of Economic and Administrative Sciences Research Methods in Social Sciences, Izmir 2015.

Demir, Osman Demir, "tesânüd", *Islamic Encyclopedia of Diyanet*, IL, 2011, pp. 526–527.

ed-Dûrî, Abdülazîz, "Divan", *Islamic Encyclopedia of Diyanet*, Istanbul 1994, IX/377–381.

Ebu Dâvud, Süleyman b. el-Eş'as es-Sicistani, (A.D. 889), *Sünen*, Çağrı Publications, Istanbul 1982.

Erdoğan, Mehmet, *Dictionary of Islamic Law and Legal Terminology*, Rağbet Publications, (Publication date and place not available).

Erdoğan, Suat, "Fıqh on Zakat Collection by Government", *Journal of Islamic Legal Research*, 2016, Issue: 28, pp. 417–434.

Eren, Paydaş, "The Institution of Kasâme in Terms of Sociology of the Law", *Marmara University Faculty of Law Journal of Legal Research*, 21, (pp. 595–614).

Erol, Ayten, "World Family Summits", Activity Evaluation, *Kırıkkale University Journal of the Faculty of Islamic Sciences (KİİFAD)*, c. 1, Issue: 1, 2016, pp. 75–82.

Erol, Ayten, "Gaining Moral Values from an Islamic Jurisprudence Perspective", *Kırıkkale University Journal of Social Sciences (KUSBD)*, July 2016, 6, Issue: 2, pp. 229–254.

Erol, Ayten, "The Societal Change and Progression Methodology of Islamic Law in Relation to Maslahah", Editor: Ayten Erol, *Maslahat in Islamic Sciences*, Gece Kitaplığı Publishing House, Ankara 2017, (pp. 13–39).

Erturhan, Sabri, "The Moral Principles that Give Body to Islamic Commercial Law", *Journal of Islamic Legal Research*, Islamic Economics Special Issue, XVI, Issue: 16, Konya 2010, pp. 213–246.

Encyclopedia of Miracles in Coran and Sunnah "Social Solidarity and Social Security in Islam" Translated by: Yasmin Muhammed Moslem, www. quran-m.com/firas/en1, (03.05. 2018).

Esed, Muhammed, *Manner of Administration in Islam*, Trans.: M. Beşir Eryarsoy, Yöneliş Publications, Istanbul, (publication date not available).

Eskicioğlu, Osman, "Economic System in Islam", *Journal of Islamic Legal Research*, Issue: 16, 2010, pp. 35–46.

Euzeby, Alain, "Social Protection: Values to Be defended", *International Social Security Review*, vol. 57, 2/2004

ez-Zerkâ, M. Ahmet, A. Muhammed, Abdülaziz en-Neccâr, *Economics, Banking, and Insurance in Islamic Thought*, Trans.: Hayreddin Karaman, İz Publishing House, Istanbul 2017.

ez-Zuhaylî, Vehbe, *Nazariyyetü'd-Damân ve Ahkâmu'l-Mes'ûliyyeti'l-Medeniyye*, Dımaşk 1402/1982.

ez-Zuhaylî, Vehbe, *el-Vecîz fi Usûli'l-Fıkh*, Dâru'l-Fıkh, Dımeşk-Suriye 1431/2010.

Fayda, Mustafa, "Fey", *Islamic Encyclopedia of Diyanet*, 1995, XII/511-513.

Garcia, A. Bonilla, J.V. Gruat, *Social Protection – Version 1.0*, International Labour Office, Geneva 2003.

Gazzâlî, Ebû Hâmid Muhammed b. Muhammed, *İhyâu Ulûmi'd-Dîn*, (Publisher not available), Beirut 1412/1992, I–V.

Gazzâlî, Ebû Hâmid Muhammed b. Muhammed (A.D. 505/1111), *el-Müstesfâ min İlmi'l-Usûl*, (Publisher not available) , Beirut 1993 (I–II).

Gerek, Nüvit Gerek, A. İlhan Oral, *Social Security Law*, Anadolu University Web-Ofset Publications, Eskişehir 2004. https://books.google.com.tr/books? id=Sqkv2okt95YC&pg=PR1&lpg=PR1&dq=N%C3%BCvit+Gerek,+A.+%C4%B0lhan+Oral+sosyal+G%C3%BCvenlik+Hukuku&source=bl&ots=0611 9rRPVR&sig=M9MAbxOBcPloV3Sh-_xTxo2h65A&hl=tr&sa=X&ved=2ahU KEwjehaCY_bzdAhXll4sKHRNFACoQ6AEwBHoECAYQAQ#v=onepage& q&f=false .

Gülmez, Mesut, "Social Security or Social Protection? The "First" Contrarian Thoughts on International Size and Evolution," *Social Human Rights International Symposium*, VII, p. 117) http://www.sosyalhaklar.net/2015/bildiriler/gulmez2.pdf (12.04.2018)

Gümüşhanevî, Ahmed Ziyaeddin, (A.D.1893), *Râmuzu'l-Ehâdis*, İstanbul 1982.

Günay, Hacı Mehmet, The Culture of Poverty as an Element of Risk in the Realization of the Main Objectives of Religion, *Journal of Islamic Legal Research*, Issue: 11, Konya 2008, (pp. 303–316).

Günay, Hacı Mehmet, "Muhammed Tâhir b. Âşûr'un Makâsıd Anlayışı", Ahmet Yaman, *Intentions and Judicial Opinion, Philosophy of Islamic Law Araştırmaları*, İFAV, 3rd Edition, Istanbul 2017.

Gündüzöz, Güldane, *The Motif of Food in Bektashi Culture*, Atatürk Cultural Center Publications, Ankara 2015.

Güzel, Ali; Okur, Ali Rıza *Social Security Law*, Beta Publications, Istanbul 1990.

Hallâf, Abdulvehhâb, *İlmu Usûli'l-Fıkh*, Mektebetü'd-Da'veti'l-İslâmiyye, Şebâbü'l-Ezher, Egypt (publication date not available).

Hanbel, Ahmed b., *el-Müsned*, Çağrı Publication, Istanbul 1982 I-VI.

Haçkalı, Abdurrahman, "El-İzz b. Abdisselâmda Intent-Judicial Opinion Relationship", Ahmet Yaman, in the book of *Intent and Judicial Opinion*, Marmara University Faculty of Divinity Foundation Publications, Istanbul 2017, pp. 285–305.

ILO, "Report of the Committee on Social Security", Sixth item on the agenda: Social security – Issues, challenges and prospects. International Labour Conference, Provisional Record Eighty-ninth Session, Geneva, 2001.

ILO, "Social Protection as a Productive Factor", Governing Body, Committee on Employment and Social Policy (GB.294/ESP/4 294th Session), Geneva, 2005.

İbn Abdisselâm, İzzüddîn Abdilaziz, *el-Kavâidu'l-Kübrâ (Kavâidü'l-Ahkâm fî Mesâlihi'l-Enâm (Kavâid)*, I-II, Dâru'l-Kalem, Dımeşk, (publication date not available).

İbn Âşûr, Muhammed Tâhir, *Philosophy of Islamic Law: The Problem of Purpose*, (Trans. İbn Kayyim, Abdullah b. Muhammed b. Ebi Bekr el-Cevziyye, (A.D. 751/1350), *İ'lâmu'l-Muvakkîn an Rabbi'l-Âlemîn*, Dâru'l-İbn Cevziyye, Riyad 1423 (I-VII).

İbn Âşûr, Muhammed Tahir, *Makâsıdüş-Şerîati'l-İslâmiyye*, Daru'n-Nefâes, Umman, (publication date not available).

İbn Âşûr, Muhammed Tahir, *Philosophy of Islamic Law, The Problem of Intent*, Translators: Mehmet Erdoğan, Vecdi Akyüz, Rağbet Publications, Istanbul 2013.

İbn Ebî Şeybe, Ebû Bekr b. Abdillah b. Muhammed el-Kûfî (A.D. 235), *Kitâbu'l-Musannef fil-Ehâdîs ve'l-Âsâr*, I–VII, Riyad 1409.

İbn Haldûn, Abdurrahman (A.D. 808/1405), *Mukaddime*, I–III, Kahire 1401.

İbn Mâce, Ebû Abdullah Muhammed b. Yezîd, el-Kazvînî, *es-Sünen*, Çağrı Puplications, İstanbul 1982.

İbn Manzur, Cemalüddîn Muhammed b. Mukrem, *Lisânü'l-Arab*, Dâru Sadr, Beyrut, (publication date not available).

Kapar, Recep, Greater Social Protection for Social Justice, II, National Social Policy Congress (24–26 November 2006), Ankara. www.disk.org.tr, www.sosyalkoruma.net

Karaman, Hayreddin, "Justice", (Islamic Law), *Islamic Encyclopedia of Diyanet*, 1988, (I/343–344).

Karaman, Hayreddin, *Comparative Islamic Law*, Bayrak Printing, Istanbul 1991, (I–III).

Karaman, Hayreddin, *Islamic Legal History*, İz Publishing, Istanbul 1999.

Karaman, Hayreddin, *Issues of the Day in the Light of Islam1-2-3*, İz Publishing House, Istanbul 2002.

Karaman, Hayreddin, *Islamic Law in the Face of New Developments*, İz Publishing House, Istanbul 2004.

Karaman, Hayreddin, "Social Justice", https://www.yenisafak.com/yazarlar/hayrettinkaraman/sosyal-adalet-2038715. (12.03. 2018)

Kastalânî, Ebû'l-Abbâs Şihâbuddîn Ahmed b. Muhammed (A.D. 923), *İrşâdu's-Sârî li Şerhi Sahîhi'l-Buhârî*, , (Muslim side commentary by Nevevî), Beirut, 1305,I-X.

Kaya, Pir Ali, "*An Evaluation on the Theoretical Framework of Social Justice*", Prof. Dr. N. Ekin'e Armağan, *Istanbul University Journal of the Faculty of Economics*, Istanbul, p. 229–240.

Kılıç, Ramazan- Şahin Çetinkaya, "Social Aid Strategies and a Model Recommendation in the Struggle with Poverty in Turkey", *Dumlupınar University Journal of Social Sciences*, Issue: 34, December 2012, (pp. 93–114).

Koca, Ferhat, "An Evaluation of Maslahat-ı Mürsele ve Necmeddin et-Tûfî's Views on this Issue in Islamic Law,", *İLAM Journal of Research*, Issue: 1, January–June 1996.

Koca, Ferhat, "Tûfî" article, *Islamic Encyclopedia of Diyanet*, XLI, 2012, pp. 327–330.

Köse, Murtaza, "The Concept of Social Policy and Ömer B. Abdülaziz's Social Policy", *Atatürk University Journal of the Faculty of Divinity*, Issue: 34, Erzurum 2010.

Köse, Saffet, "The Summit of Prestige Because of the Humanity of Humans in Muslim Thought", *Journal of Islamic Legal Research*, Konya 2009, Issue: 14, pp. 49–66.

Köse, Saffet, "Is it Law or Morality? Research in the Context of the Religion-Morals-Law Relationship from Islam Viewpoint", *Journal of Islamic Legal Research*, Konya 2011, Issue: 17.

Köse, Saffet, *Introduction to Islamic Law*, Hikmetevi Publications, Step Publishing Tan Co., Istanbul 2014.

Kurtûbî, Muhammed b. Ahmed, (A.D. 671–1273), *el-Câmi'li Ahkâmi'l-Kur'ân*, (Publisher not available), Egypt 1935/1950.

Mahmud, Abdullatif Al-i, *et-Te'min el-İctimaî fi Dav'iş-Şeriati'l-İslâmiyye*, Darünnefais, Beirut, 1994.

Midgley, James , "Challenges Facing Social Security", *Challenges to Social Security*, Ed.: James Midgley, Martin B. Tracy, Greenwood Publishing Group, Connecticut, 1996.

Müslim, İbn el-Haccâc el-Kuşeyrî (A.D. 875), *Sahîhu Müslim (el-Câmiu's-Sahih)*, Çağrı Yayınları, İstanbul 1981.

Okur, Kâşif Hamdi, *The Example of Surety of Social Responsibility in Islamic Law*, Center for Islamic Studies (İSAM) Publications, Istanbul 2017.

Özdemir, Süleyman, "A New Understanding in the Provision of Social Welfare: "The Welfare Mix" and Welfare Providing Institutions". http://eski. bingol.edu.tr/media/154992/dddtamami.pdf (15.10. 2017)

Özen, Şükrü, "İstislâh", *Islamic Encyclopedia of Diyanet*, 2001, XXIII/383–388.

Öztürk, Şenol, "The Approach of New Social Risk in Social Protection," *Social Policy Conferences*, Issue: 66–67, 2014/1–2, (pp. 43–74). http://dergipark.gov. tr/iusskd (01.02.2018)

Paydaş Eren, "The Institution of Kasâme in Terms of Sociology of the Law", *Marmara University Faculty of Law Journal of Legal Research*, 21, (pp. 595–614).

Sağlam, Hadi, "Methods That Provide Dynamism to Islamic Law in the Face of Modern Problems", http://www.akademiktarih.com/tarih-anabilim-dal/2026-osmanl-aratrmalar/osmanlkuki-yap/28845-cada-problemler-karisinda-slam-hukukuna-dnamzm-salayan-metotlar.html (22.05.2017)

Sağlam, Hadi, "Religious Officials' Guide to Social Security." http://kidep.net/ wp-content/uploads/din-gorevlileri-rehberi.pdf (15.03.2017)

Sağlam, Hadi, "The Institutions of Social Security and Techniques of Social Cooperation and Solidarity in Islamic Legal History." http://www.e-akademi. org/incele.asp? 1242645203&url=makaleler/hsaglam-2.htm (12.03.2016)

Sağlam, Hadi, "Are Reparations in Islamic Legal History the Insurance of Today?", *Cumhuriyet University Journal of the Faculty of Divinity*, 2011, vol. 15, Issue: 1, pp. (265–292).

Sağlam, Hadi, "A Summary Analysis of the Historical Roots of Today's Social Security Institution", *Erzincan University Journal of the Institute of Social Sciences (ERZSOSDE)*, IX–I, 2016, pp. 131–142.

Sargın, Ebru, The Contributions of Social Cooperation and Solidarity Foundations on a Country's Economy, Namık Kemal University Institute of Social Sciences, *Unprinted Graduate Thesis*, Tekirdağ 2017.

Sargın, İzzet, The Entirety of Human Rights and the State, *Notices of the Human Rights and Religion Symposium*, 15–17 May 2009, Çanakkale Onsekiz Mart University Publications, Çanakkale 2010.

Seyyar, Ali, *Social Policy Terminology*, Sakarya Bookstore, Adapazarı, 2nd Edition, 2008, relevant articles. http://www.idefix.com/kitap/sosyal-siyaset-terimleri-ansiklopedik-sozluk-ciltli-ali-seyyar/tanim.asp?sid=V8XK5BH8SS 5SHOXTB1CV. (09.12.2014)

Scripture/Torah, Scripture Company, Istanbul 1981.

Scripture /Bible, Scripture Company ('Together with the Torah), Istanbul 1981.

Suyutî, Abdurrahmân b. Ebî Bekr, (A.D. 1505), *el-Camiu's-Sağir*, (Publisher not available) Dımeşk, 1986.

Syed, İbrahim, "Social Security in Islam", http://www.irfi.org/articles/articles_251_300/social_security_in_islam.htm (11.05.2017).

Şatıbî, Ebu İshak İbrahim b. Musa, (A.D. 790/*1388*), *el-Muvâfakât fî Usûli'ş-Şerîa*, Dâru İbn Affân, Saudi Arabia 1997.

Şeker, Mehmet Şeker, *Institutes of Social Solidarity in Islam*, Ministry of Religious Affairs Publications/240, Public Books/76, Ankara 2007.

Şen, Yusuf, "An Evaluation on the Social Dimension of Foundations in Islamic Law", *Journal of Islamic Legal Research*, Issue: 17, 2011, pp. 415–426.

Şenocak, Hasan, "An Evaluation of the Components that Form the Social Security System in Light of the Historical Process". http://dergipark.ulakbim.gov.tr/iusskd/article/viewFile/1023000094/1023000089 (29.12.2017).

Şimşek, H. Ahmet, A Sociological Approach to the Institute of Alms in Islam, *Unprinted Graduate Thesis*, Selçuk University, Institute of Social Sciences, Konya 1994.

Tabakoğlu, Ahmet, "Islamic Economics as a Science", *Journal of Islamic Legal Research*, Issue:16, 2010, pp. 11–34.

Taberânî, Ebû'l-Kâsım Süleyman b. Ahmed b. Eyyûb, (A.D. 360), *el-Mu'cemu'l-Kebîr*, (Publisher not available), Mosul 1404/1983, I–XX.

Taftâzânî, Sa'duddîn Mes'ûd b. Ömer, (A.D. 792/1390), *Şerhu'l-Ehâdîsi'l-Erba'în li'n-Nevevî, (together with the Şerhu'l-Ehâdîsi'l-Erba'în belonging to Birgivî and Akkirmânî)*, Dersaâdet Publications (publication date and place not available).

Taştan, Osman, "Human Rights and Religions Education through Islamic Legal Theory", E. Asla and M. Rausch (Eds.) *Religious Education*, Springer Fachmedien Wiesbaden GmbH, Wiesbaden Germany 2018.

Temel, Nihat *Assistance as Social Security Institutions in the Quran*, Emre Press, Istanbul 2000.

Temür, Yusuf, "The Institution of Negative Taxes in the Scope of the Welfare State and of Alms in the Economy of Islam", *BJSS Balkan Journal of Social Sciences*, *vol*.6 Issue: 12.

The Way of the Quran, Constructive Volume: 1, p.385–386. https://kuran.diyanet.gov.tr/tefsir/Bakara-suresi/252/245-ayet-tefsiri

Tirmizî, Muhammed b. İsa b. Serve, (A.D. 892), *el-Camiu's-Sahih, Sünenü't-Tirmizî*, Egypt 1975.

Tokol, Aysen, *Social Policy*, 2nd Edition, Uludağ University, Ceylan Publishing, Bursa 1997.

Tuncay, A. Can, *Social Security Law Courses*, Beta Basım Publishing Distribution Co., Istanbul 1984.

Turkish Language Institute Big Turkish Dictionary, http://tdk.gov.tr/index.php?option=com_bts&arama=kelime&guid=TDK.GTS.586a8503dacf31.50664163 (02.01.2017)

Ulvân, Abdullah Nâsıh, *Social Solidarity in Islam*, Trans.: İsmail Kaya, Uysal Bookstore, Sebat Ofset Press, Konya 1985.

Ulvân, Abdullah Nâsıh, *The Social Security System in Islam*, Trans.: Nizamettin Saltan, Bakanlar Publishing Ltd. Co., Erzurum 2001.

Ündemir, Yasemin Göknur, *Forecasting the Important Variables of Social Security Through Time Series Analysis* 2011, *Social Security Expertise Thesis*, Presidency of Turkish Social Security Institution, 2009.

Yaman, Ahmet, "On the Principles of Purposeful Judicial Opinion or Intent/Theological Interpretation Administration in Terms of Islamic Legal Science", *Intent and Judicial Opinion*, Marmara University, Faculty of Divinity Foundation Publications, Istanbul 2017.

Yaran, Rahmi, *The Concept and Institutionalization of Need in Islamic Law*, Marmara University, Faculty of Divinity Foundation Publications, Istanbul 2007.

Yavuz, Yunus Vehbi, "Interpreting Intent", *Journal of Islamic Legal Research*, Issue: 8, Mehir Foundation Publications, Konya 2006.

Yay, Serdar, "The Social State in Turkey in the Historical Process", *Journal of 21st Century Education and Society*, Issue: 9, Winter2014.

Yazgan, Turan, "Alms in Terms of Social Security", *Journal of Turkic World Research*, 1, Issue: 6, Uludağ Printing, Istanbul 1980.

Yazgan, Turan, *Turkish Social Security System and Issues (TSGSM)*, Foundation of Research in the Turkish World, Istanbul 1981.

Yazıbaşı, Muhammed Ali, "Moral Education and Instruction from Classical Ottoman to II. Mesrutiyet Period in Ottoman", *Journal of Human and Societal Sciences Research*, 2014, vol.3, Issue: 4, (pp. 761–780).

Yazıcı, Nesimi, "The Social Market Economic and its Perception in Islam", Çalıştay, Ankara 2010. http://www.kas.de/wf/doc/kas_23417-1522-12-30.pdf?110816144640. (14.03.2018)

Yıldırım, Adem, "An Overview of the Makasidu'sh-Sharia in Islamic Law Literatüre", *Maslahat in Islamic Sciences*, Editor: Ayten Erol, Gece Kitaplığı Publishing House, Ankara 2017, p: 149–172.

Yılmaz, Faruk, *The Economy of Islam and Social Security System*, Compilation: Ömer Chapra, Hurşid Ahmed, Faruk Yılmaz, Abdurrahman Şah, Turkish-English Bibliographies: Sabahaddin Zaim, M.N. Sıddikî, Marifet Publications/46, Yaylacık Press, Istanbul 1991.

Yiğit, İsmail, "Ömer b. Abdülazîz", *Islamic Encyclopedia of Diyanet*, Istanbul 2007, XXXIV/53–54.

Zeydan, Abdülkerim, *el-Veciz fi Usuli'l-Fıkıh*, Dersaâdet, Istanbul, (Publication date not available)

Electronic References

Hayreddin Karaman, http://www.hayrettinkaraman.net/makale/0609.htm. (25.07.2017).

https://www.unicef.org/turkey/udhr/_gi17.html (12.10.2017)

https://www.tbmm.gov.tr/anayasa/anayasa_2011.pdf

Chapter XI. *Ekli Cetvel.* http://www.ilo.org/ankara/conventions-ratified-by-turkey/WCMS_377270/lang--tr/index.htm (25.09.2017)

http://www.yenisafak.com/yazarlar/hayrettinkaraman/yoksullara-yardim-nasil yapilmalidir-15681. (04.03.2018)

Tekâfül, "What is Islamic Insurance?", http://tekaful.net/?page_id=148 (20.02.2017)

Back Cover

The law is for people. At the forefront of the characteristics of a successful legal system come responding to the expectations and meeting the needs of people and providing the social protection of people by creating rights and justice among them.

According to Islamic law, the right to live is a primary human right. This right, granted by God, begins with the right of people to come to Earth and is thus revealed with God's creation of man. According to Islamic law, social protection carries great importance in terms of meeting the needs regarding the preservation of *zarûriyyât-ı hamse* (life, property, intellect, lineage, religion), whose protection is imperative, primarily for the life and maintenance of assets of all humans and for the realization of the right to life.

According to Islamic law, regardless of religion, the goal is the provision of social justice, social peace, and social protection throughout the world, by precluding all kinds of disorder and conflict that may occur in society with the prevention of risks and dangers to the preservation of these values in question, the development of the personality, and the elimination of need for all of humanity. In this context, all people are under the umbrella of social protection, according to Islamic law.

Islamic law aims for the social development of society by making dominant feelings of tawhid/unity, justice, brotherhood, social solidarity, sharing, and cooperation for the creation of a social order that ensures people fulfill their duties of servitude for God and for sustainable development.

In order for social protection to be able to be provided all over the world, according to Islamic law, the approaches and fundamental principles regarding the *outlook* on *man, property, and life* of the religion of Islam must be known and implemented. However, the implementation of these fundamental principles and approaches carry importance to the degree of the religiosity of people and their dependence on religious provisions and will reach the desired results.

*9 7 8 3 6 3 1 7 5 9 1 3 4 *